D0850249

The Guest from
the Future

THE GUEST FROM THE FUTURE

Anna Akhmatova and Isaiah Berlin

GYÖRGY DALOS

With the collaboration of ANDREA DUNAI

Translated from the German by ANTONY WOOD

FARRAR, STRAUS AND GIROUX

New York

Farrar, Straus and Giroux
19 Union Square West, New York 10003

Library of Congress Cataloging-in-Publication Data
Dalos, György.
    The guest from the future : Anna Akhmatova and Isaiah Berlin /
György Dalos ; with the collaboration of Andrea Dunai ; translated
from the German by Antony Wood. — 1st American ed.
        p. cm.
    Includes bibliographical references and index.
    ISBN 0-374-16727-3 (alk. paper)
    1. Akhmatova, Anna Andreevna, 1889-1966—Friends and associates.
2. Berlin, Isaiah, Sir.   3. Poets, Russian—20th century Biography.
I. Dunai, Andrea.   II. Title
PG3476.A324Z59   1999
891.71'42—dc21
[B]   99-32516

To the memory of Naum Isayevich Grebnev

Contents

Illustrations

The author and publishers would like to thank the following for permission to reproduce illustrations: the Estate of Anna Akhmatova (p. 30); Anatoly Nayman (pp. 22, 29, 68, 161); J. Russell & Sons (p. 39).

Preface

This book is the story of a single night, the night of Isaiah Berlin's visit to Anna Akhmatova in Leningrad in November 1945, and its unfortunate consequences, and is told mainly from Akhmatova's viewpoint. It is a love story, the story of a love that became a focal point in the life of the poet, giving meaning to events that preceded and followed it. And since the relationship between Akhmatova and Berlin developed under the watchful eyes of the KGB, the story is also a parable about Soviet life, its 'normality' and absurdities, about the intricate relationship between literature and the power of the state.

This book is not a biography of Anna Akhmatova, nor is it a work of literary criticism. Any account of Isaiah Berlin's life and work is even further from my purpose – I am not qualified to assess him as a thinker and historian of ideas, and his private persona I glimpse only intermittently through the interstices of Akhmatova's life and poetry. The meeting on that night was important to him, but not fateful; Akhmatova's subsequent life and work, however, were decisively affected by it.

As a young poet and student at Moscow University in the 1960s I had read some of Akhmatova's poems that were then available, and was familiar with the Party Resolution of August 1946 and Zhdanov's speech in which he had branded Akhmatova as 'a nun and a whore'. Akhmatova, however, had made no profound impact on me at this time. Only some fifteen years later did I come to appreciate the mesmerizing power of her language, but even then I felt no special closeness to her as a poet. I had the impression that Akhmatova would allow no one close to her; she disliked using the familiar form of address.

I do not know English, and it was not until after 1989, when translations of his books began to appear in Eastern Europe, that I first heard of Isaiah Berlin. I thought of him as an important British thinker who had possibly died long ago.

In the summer of 1975, in the writers' colony of Peredelkino near Moscow, I met Lydia Chukovskaya. At that time this sixty-eight-year-old writer and publisher's editor had been marginalized by the Party as a result of her support for fellow writers who were being persecuted by the state. Once we had exchanged greetings she mentioned to me what was then her chief anxiety: owing to her poor eyesight she was afraid of inadvertently shaking hands with writers who had participated in the smear campaign against Solzhenitsyn and Sakharov. She told me she was working on a journal of her friendship with Akhmatova.

I was something of a dissident at this time, my considerably belated Sturm und Drang period. Emotionally I was finding myself more and more distant from the Soviet Union. My political activities were focused on Hungary and Central Europe, and my writing was increasingly concerned with the German-speaking regions. At the same time I had a bad conscience about Russian culture, the country and its people – I felt guilty. I had spent the most important years of my youth in Russia, and formed many close connections among its remarkable and warm-hearted people. Drawn to Russia by many personal ties, I have long been an assiduous observer of its political and everyday life.

I had also been seized with another form of nostalgia –

for the golden period of my literary beginnings. My longing was not so much for the poetry I wrote in my youth, which from today's viewpoint seems to me less than impressive. What I felt far more strongly was a renewed, belated surge of the teenage schoolboy's ambition to ally himself with the indisputably great. I wanted, as at the age of seventeen, to read poetry once more, to talk about it, not with any idea of cultural development, but simply because I couldn't live without it.

In spring 1993 I attended a seminar on 'State Security and Literature' organized by the Heinrich Böll Foundation in Moscow. A retired KGB general, Oleg Kalugin, gave a paper on the Anna Akhmatova file, mentioning Berlin's night visit to Akhmatova's flat in Leningrad. The operational file, said to hold 900 pages in all, has since disappeared – I assume someone planned or still plans to capitalize on it. This occasion apart, the former general seems not to have attached any special importance to the subject of Anna Akhmatova. His memoirs were published in 1995; garrulous and superficial, they contain no reference to Akhmatova at all. His quotations from the secret file, however, made me sit up and take notice.

I looked through the latest editions of Akhmatova published in Russia for poems connected with the 'Guest from the Future'. I noticed how lines and words I knew or thought I knew seemed to flash out and take on an unusual density and entirely new layers of meaning. I myself changed too: previously only an occasional reader of Akhmatova, in a few short weeks I became an ardent admirer of her poetry.

This book has been written on the basis of archival material, reminiscences of contemporary witnesses, and numerous conversations. Lydia Chukovskaya spoke to me at length shortly before her death. I had telephone conversations with Emma Gerstein and Anatoly Nayman. I visited Britain to interview Isaiah Berlin on the subject of his essay 'Meetings with Russian Writers in 1945 and 1956' contained in his book *Personal Impressions*. Especially fruitful was a conversation with Professor Harry Shukman, who was a member of the British student delegation that visited Leningrad in spring 1954 and met Anna Akhmatova there. The Hungarian journalist Andrea Dunai assisted me in my researches in Moscow, and at interviews conducted in Oxford and London, as well as with the sifting of material, and I am much indebted to her.

To Elsbeth Zylla, with whom, in close intellectual symbiosis, I have translated this my eighth book into German, I am especially grateful not only for her linguistic and stylistic help but also for valuable advice on content. And I should like to express thanks to Franziska Groszer and Gabriele Dietze for their attentive reading of my manuscript.

I particularly thank the following for their support and stimulating suggestions while I was writing this book:

Simon Bailey, Oxford; the late Sir Isaiah Berlin, Oxford; Irina Bojko, Chernovits; the late Lydia Chukovskaya, Moscow; Yelena Chukovskaya, Moscow; Emma Gerstein, Moscow; Henry Hardy, Oxford; Michael Ignatieff, London; Lyudmila Karachkina, Simferopol; Lev Kopelev, Cologne; Gennady Kostyrchenko, Moscow; Anatoly Nayman, Moscow; Henning Ritter, Frankfurt/M; Harry Shukman, Oxford; Lyudmila Shuravlyova, Simferopol; and Zsuzsanna Zsohár, London.

Preface to the English Language Edition

In the course of preparation of the English edition of this book I have corrected some factual slips in the original edition and have also made amendments in the light of further inspection of material quoted, sometimes quoting in more detail. I have also added an Appendix consisting of a memorandum concerning Anna Akhmatova, dated 15 August 1946, from the head of the Leningrad branch of the Ministry of State Security to Andrey Zhdanov; and extended the original coverage under the Chronologies and Select Bibliography to include recent English-language publications.

Anna Akhmatova's verse is quoted mostly in the English translations by Judith Hemschemeyer (*The Complete Poems of Anna Akhmatova*, Canongate Books, Edinburgh and Zephyr Press, Somerville, MA, 1990; © Judith Hemschemeyer, various dates) and by Richard McKane (*Selected Poems*, Bloodaxe Books, 1989; © Richard McKane, 1969, 1989), with occasional slight revisions, by kind permission of the publishers.

Extracts from 'Meetings with Russian Writers in 1945 and 1956' (© Isaiah Berlin, 1980) in *Personal Impressions* by Isaiah Berlin are reproduced by permission of Random House UK Limited. Letters written by Isaiah Berlin are quoted by permission of the Trustees of the Isaiah Berlin Literary Trust. Crown copyright material in the Public

Record Office is reproduced by permission of the Controller of Her Majesty's Stationery Office.

Sources of all other quotations are as listed at the end of the book. Quotations of non-English-language material are translated from original sources by Antony Wood except where otherwise stated.

G.D.
March 1998

The Guest from
the Future

1 *The Meeting*

Isaiah Berlin, First Secretary at the British Embassy in Moscow, thirty-five years of age, was not a career diplomat. Before the war he had been a scholar and then a lecturer at Oxford. In the 1930s he had established an academic reputation with a monograph on Marx. During the war he had worked for the Ministry of Information in New York and then written highly praised reports on American public opinion for the British Embassy in Washington (for which he was later appointed CBE). While during the war his critical and analytical abilities had performed an important service for the United Kingdom, after it his excellent knowledge of Russian and special knowledge of circumstances inside the Soviet Union proved particularly useful.

In the course of a brilliant post-war academic career at Oxford, Isaiah Berlin was Professor of Social and Political Theory, founder and first president of Wolfson College, and author of a number of seminal essays on political theory and literature. He was knighted in 1957. Born in Riga in 1909, he was the son of a Russian-Jewish timber merchant. When he was seven years old his family moved to St Petersburg, where they remained for the next three years. When after the October Revolution they returned to a now independent Latvia and then emigrated to England, the young Berlin took with him deep and lasting memories of his Russian homeland. His wide reading of Russian literature ensured that he never forgot his mother-tongue, and he continued to speak it with no trace of an accent.

Meeting him in London in 1995, I even detected Moscow slang of the 1990s in his Russian.

The prospect of an official job in the country of his birth filled Berlin with eager anticipation. 'I have like all the Three Sisters been saying "To Moscow, to Moscow",' he wrote on 12 May 1945 from Washington to a British diplomatic friend, 'for goodness knows how long, and probably have exaggerated ideas about how exciting it all will be. I shall arrive armed with every resource for the maintaining of civilized life that I am allowed to bring by air ... Insecticides, shoe leather, a sealskin cap, and goodness knows what.'

The life of a diplomat in the Soviet capital proved not only 'civilized', but extremely entertaining. Berlin expressed his elation at being there in a number of letters written soon after his arrival. 'I am fascinated by everything,' he reported on 19 September. 'The conversations in the street & theatres particularly. I had forgotten that such emotions & expressions existed.' In these first days he saw Tchaikovsky's *Eugene Onegin* at the Bolshoy Theatre, and discovered Russian mushroom soups and *pirozhki* (small pies). According to a letter written on 11 October, these gastronomic and cultural delights amounted almost to a whole way of life in themselves: 'I go to the theatre or opera practically every night, & eat hot borshch at home at 11 p.m. & go to bed at 11.30 ...'

Here, surely, lies much of the explanation for Berlin's enormous enthusiasm for Russia: in the experience of rediscovery. Certain culinary pleasures no doubt awakened memories from childhood, while on the Moscow stage characters from classic works read long ago suddenly assumed flesh and blood. Exchanges heard in the street, the song of a Red Army unit marching by, a chambermaid's chatter in diplomatic quarters must have reminded him that although he did not belong to this world, he was connected with it far more strongly than he had suspected, by one indestructible bond – that of language.

Berlin was soon preparing for a trip to Leningrad in September, the reason for which lay at least partly in his love of books.

> I had heard that books in Leningrad, in what in the Soviet Union were called 'antiquarian bookshops', cost a good deal less than in Moscow; the terrible mortality and the possibility of bartering books for food during the siege of that city had led to a flow of books, especially of the old [pre-revolutionary] intelligentsia, into government bookshops . . . I should have done my best to go to Leningrad in any case, for I was eager to see again the city in which I had spent four years of my childhood; the lure of books added to my desire.

Leningrad promised to be every bit as entertaining as Moscow. Berlin booked tickets for Tchaikovsky's *Sleeping Beauty*, Glinka's recently rehabilitated national opera *Ivan Susanin* (formerly entitled *A Life for the Tsar*) and the ballet *Gayane* by the Armenian Aram Khachaturian – all obligatory for foreign visitors to the city. Berlin stayed at the Astoria Hotel, where the cuisine surely did not disappoint him. He made the visit with Brenda Tripp, a chemical specialist with diplomatic status working in the Soviet Union for the British Council.

Personal contacts with writers were not planned as part of Berlin's work. He had been prepared, rather, for meeting a series of grey apparatchiks. He had one personal request to fulfil, however, besides his official duties. Boris Pasternak's two sisters, who lived in England, had asked him before his departure to take a pair of boots to their brother in Moscow. This mission was to prove highly productive for Berlin, resulting in a warm and lasting friendship with the author of *Doctor Zhivago*. At diplomatic receptions Berlin had already met a number of Russian intellectuals, including the film director Sergey Eisenstein and the children's author and translator from English, Samuil Marshak.

Maurice Bowra, a classicist of wide literary interests and Warden of Wadham College, who had translated some of Anna Akhmatova's poems, took an interest in Berlin's posting to Russia. The two often corresponded about contemporary Russian poets. 'Mandelstam is, I am pretty certain, dead,' wrote Bowra in the summer of 1945, 'starved by being put bottom on the list of food tickets because of his disloyal verses. What about Akhmatova? Said to be alive in Leningrad.' In his reply Berlin told Bowra the little he knew: 'Akhmatova lives in Leningrad and is very inaccessible on account of being a survival of an older day, although not exactly a Fascist beast.' This state of knowledge of contemporary Russian writers on the part of two Western experts on Russian literature was symptomatic of the most impassable communications barrier erected in modern history, the Iron Curtain, already in place well before Churchill popularized the term on 5 March 1946. Osip Mandelstam had been dead seven years.

In *Personal Impressions* (1980) Berlin recalls how in the private inner room of the Writers' Bookshop on the Nevsky Prospekt, 'the object of his journey' to Leningrad, he and Brenda Tripp fell into conversation with a man 'turning over the leaves of a book of poems'. This was in fact the literary scholar V.N. Orlov, who happened to be preparing two selections of Akhmatova's poems for publication. In the middle of their conversation, which touched on the terrible years of the Siege, Berlin asked him about the fate of writers in Leningrad. 'You mean Zoshchenko and Akhmatova?' Orlov replied, as if no other names among two hundred writers of the city were worth mentioning. 'Is Akhmatova still alive?' asked Berlin. 'Akhmatova, Anna Andreyevna? . . . Why yes, of course. She lives not far from here on the Fontanka [Canal], in Fontannyy Dom [Fountain House]; would you like to meet her?' 'It was as if I had suddenly been invited to meet Miss Christina Rossetti,' recalls Berlin; 'I could hardly speak: I mumbled that I should indeed like to meet her.' Orlov telephoned Akhmatova and arranged a meeting at three o'clock in the afternoon of the same day. Brenda Tripp was unable to come, being otherwise engaged.

Berlin and Orlov left the bookshop and, in Berlin's words, 'turned left, crossed the Anichkov Bridge and turned left again, along the embankment of the Fontanka.' Soon they stood in front of No. 34, a former palace belonging to the Sheremetev family, now known as 'Fountain House'. 'We climbed up one of the steep, dark staircases to an upper floor, and were admitted to Akhmatova's room.'

At the time of Isaiah Berlin's visit to Leningrad, both Christina Rossetti and her brother Dante Gabriel had enjoyed over half a century of well-earned immortality. The tenant at No. 34 Fontanka, however, was alive, and famous in a way that someone of comparable literary and personal standing could only be in the circumstances of an East European dictatorship.

Born in 1889, by the second decade of the twentieth century Anna Andreyevna Akhmatova was already among the most celebrated of her country's writers. In 1911 she and her first husband, the poet Nikolay Gumilyov, had founded the Acmeist group – its name derived from the Greek word *akme*, 'summit' – the aim of which was to vanquish Symbolism, which was seen as nebulous and artificial, through precise imagery and conceptual clarity. Among the group's six members was the twenty-year-old Osip Mandelstam. Paradoxically, at the

summit of the Symbolist movement they were so vehe-
mently rejecting stood a poet personally revered and loved
by Akhmatova – Aleksandr Blok.

Akhmatova was a leading figure in that pre-war flower-
ing of Russian poetry now known as the 'Silver Age'. The
daughter of a Ukrainian naval officer who settled with his
family in Tsarskoye Selo, Akhmatova spent her youth
where Pushkin had spent his. As a young woman she led
an exhilarating literary life in Tsarskoye Selo, St Petersburg
and Moscow, and with her husband Nikolay Gumilyov,
who had courted her since she was fourteen, travelled in
Western Europe after their marriage in 1910. In Paris she
met Modigliani, who made sixteen portrait drawings of
her.

Anna Akhmatova had no taste for politics. She lived
through the last years of the Silver Age, the years of the
Great War and the Revolutions writing and publishing her
poems. She had a son, Lev. Her first marriage was a free
one, and she and Gumilyov did not sever their bond of
friendship when they divorced in 1918 and she married
Vladimir Shileyko, an Assyriologist. In the wretched
conditions of the post-war years her priority was simple
survival. For a time she worked as a librarian at the
Institute of Agronomy in St Petersburg.

The turning-point in Akhmatova's life and career
occurred in August 1921. At the beginning of this month
Nikolay Gumilyov was arrested by the Cheka and after a
short secret trial executed along with sixty others. The file,
now accessible, reveals that his active participation in the
so-called 'Tagantsev Affair' – if it ever existed – was wholly
unproven. The facts of the matter are that Gumilyov had
given Vladimir Tagantsev, a Petersburg professor known to
be anti-Communist, a fairly modest sum of money in
support of dissident literature, and that he often criticized
the Bolsheviks, though never in his poetry. Such criticism

*Anna Gorenko aged fifteen, at Tsarskoye Selo. Two years later she chose
the surname 'Akhmatova', that of her Tatar great-grandmother*

was not unusual in Russian intellectual circles and frequently went unpunished at this time.

  On 7 August 1921, between the arrest and execution of
Gumilyov, Aleksandr Blok died – illness, malnutrition,
despair over the condition of Russia, and the rejection of

Gumilyov and Akhmatova with their son Lev, 1915 or 1916

his application to make a trip to Finland for medical treatment contributing to his untimely death. The loss of the
two most important persons in her life within a matter of
days was a shock from which Akhmatova never fully
recovered. It was surely one of the chief reasons why her
output was drastically reduced in the ensuing years – from
1922 to 1935 she wrote fewer poems than in 1921 alone.
The charge of 'self-willed' silence through the 1920s and
1930s, which her adversaries liked to level against her, is
pure invention.

Although Akhmatova and Gumilyov had divorced in
1918, and although no political charges were brought
against her personally, the dead man threw a long shadow.
Even after she had lived for twelve years with her third
partner, the art historian Nikolay Punin, in Fountain
House, for the Soviet authorities and the perpetrators of
the judicial murder she remained Gumilyov's widow. Her
assumption of responsibility for her former husband's

literary estate and her refusal to dissociate herself from him as a writer gave some substance to this.

Akhmatova was henceforth treated, without any further evidence, as 'politically problematic'. Whether or not she really was subject to a secret Central Committee publication ban from 1925, as many of her contemporaries and she herself believed, is difficult to prove. But it is significant that her next volume of verse, *From Six Books*, did not appear until 1940, when she was granted membership of the Writers' Union for the first time, and was withdrawn from sale and from libraries soon afterwards.

Anna Akhmatova remained isolated during these years, her circle of fellow writers being restricted to a handful of figures who were similarly treated as peripheral, or even as pariahs, Osip Mandelstam among them. At the same time, even though she could no longer publish, Akhmatova was famous, and it would appear that it was never the intention to arrest her or to mount a political trial against her. Even her friendship with Mandelstam, who was increasingly sucked into the maelstrom of the Great Terror from 1933 onwards and who died in a transit camp in 1938, was tolerated.

The continuing association with the memory of Gumilyov proved disastrous, however, for their son Lev Nikolayevich. In 1935 Fountain House was searched and he was arrested along with Nikolay Punin, but released after Akhmatova made a dramatic appeal to Stalin via friends. In March 1938, however – the last year of the Great Purges and the month in which the former Communist leader and theoretician Nikolay Bukharin was tried – Lev was rearrested, and now no intervention was effective; although he was released for military service, he was to be arrested once more in 1949 and then not released until after Khrushchev's denunciation of Stalin to a closed session of the 20th Party Congress in 1956.

Anna Akhmatova, 1927

Akhmatova's civil status became more settled at this time. She received the medal 'For the defence of Leningrad' for her broadcasts during the first months of the Siege calling on the population to resist the Germans. She was evacuated with other writers to Moscow, from where she made her way to Tashkent, publishing a short (severely censored) selection of poems there. As she prepared to return to Leningrad towards the end of the war, she saw stable and even hopeful prospects before her. She was fifty-five years old.

She also looked forward to success of a kind for which

she had long given up hope: a happy love relationship. In the late 1930s she had met a widowed Leningrad doctor, Vladimir Garshin, who had been very helpful to her when Lev was rearrested for the first time. Before Anna's evacuation Garshin, who had to stay on in the besieged city, undertook to move in with her and marry her after the war. They corresponded regularly, and the distance between them seemed to have the romantic effect of strengthening their bond.

For Akhmatova, however, this relationship was no passionate affair. While she was considering the doctor as a prospective husband, she met a Pole, Jozef Czapski, a writer and intelligence officer who was staying in the Uzbek capital as a representative of General Anders's Armija Krajowa. Czapski was the first foreigner to whom Akhmatova had talked since 1917. She dedicated a passionate poem to him, with the opening line: 'In the night we drove each other mad . . .' With Garshin, however, she wanted not to be mad, but to grow old. The prospect of life with the doctor seemed to offer her a peaceful haven, and the first real home she had had for decades.

All the friends whom Akhmatova visited when passing through Moscow in April 1944 found her radiantly happy. On the day before leaving for Leningrad she spoke to Yelena Osmyorkina of her earlier unsuccessful relationships, including her marriage to Punin. 'Then without any transition she said to me: "Do you know, I am to marry Vladimir Georgiyevich Garshin, a professor of medicine."' Another witness of her euphoria was Nina Ardova: 'in Moscow she told all her friends she was going to get married . . . She was even going to take the name "Garshina".'

Akhmatova's travelling companions on the train to Leningrad were the husband and wife Vladimir Admoni and Tamara Silman. 'We talked far into the night,' Tamara Silman recalls. 'We hadn't seen each other for more than six months. The first thing Akhmatova said was: "I am going to meet my husband!"' This was indeed the only possible course open to her, for Fountain House, the former Sheremetev Palace, was not in a habitable condition.

And then the incredible happened.

> We knew that Garshin would be there to fetch Akhmatova. And indeed, when we got out of the compartment, there on the platform stood a man who looked just like a professor ... He went up to Akhmatova, kissed her hand and said: 'Anya, we must have a talk.' They began to walk up and down the platform deep in conversation. We felt that we shouldn't go away. They didn't walk about for very long, only some five or six minutes. Then they came to a halt. Garshin kissed Akhmatova's hand again, turned round and walked off. We sensed that he really was walking right out of Akhmatova's life.
>
> Akhmatova came up to us. In a voice completely calm and collected she said: 'Everything's changed. I'm going to the Rybakovs'.'

The Rybakovs were long-standing friends of Garshin and Akhmatova. Olga Rybakova recalls that not long before Akhmatova's return to Leningrad Garshin had come to see her to tell her of a vision of his dead mother that he had had in a dream; she had forbidden him to marry Akhmatova. The dream was surely no invention, but things were rather more banal. During the tragic months of the Siege, Garshin had fallen in love with a doctor of about his own age. He felt unable to tell Akhmatova by letter, and instead waited for her to return to Leningrad when he would be able to see her in person. After their parting, he married his colleague.

Anna Akhmatova usually spoke to friends of both sexes

quite openly about marriage and relationships. Not, however, after her break-up with Garshin. Even to such a close friend as Nina Ardova she sent only two brief telegrams: 'Tell me how your health is. Warm kisses, I live alone, thank you for everything. Akhmatova.' And three weeks later: 'Garshin is mentally very ill, we have separated, you are the only one I'm telling, Anna.'

Some months later, Akhmatova moved back into Fountain House with the Punin family. The apartment, with a mere hundred square metres of floorspace, had only four rooms with shared kitchen and toilet. Besides Anna Akhmatova, the overpopulated household contained, at various times and sometimes at the same time: first, Nikolay Punin, his first wife, also called Anna, and their daughter Irina, widowed in the war, with her small daughter Anya Kaminskaya. Then there was Punin's third and current wife, Margarita. Before the war, one room was occupied by the caretaker; later Irina Punina's second husband moved in. Until his arrest in 1938 Lev Gumilyov lived at the end of the long corridor; after the war he was allowed a room of his own where he lived until his third arrest in 1949. It wasn't so much the confined space as the almost incestuous proximity of completely different family groups that must have made this communal household exceedingly difficult to live in. Above all, it was impossible ever to be really alone – the only luxury that no writer can do without.

Akhmatova tried to overcome her latest personal shock through work. *Requiem* and *Poem Without a Hero*, begun in 1936 and 1940 respectively, re-emerged as long-term projects. As a precaution against house searches and confiscation these works, which were never really completed, were entrusted to the memory of chosen friends. Some dozen of these visited Akhmatova from time to time to smuggle away in their heads corrections and additions to

Requiem, her memorial to the victims of 1937 and 1938. Not until the 1960s did this work reach typewritten form and print, in Western European countries in the first instance.

Poem Without a Hero was still being written in 1945. As she worked on the gigantic structure in which she sought to immortalize pre-revolutionary St Petersburg, the world from which she had been shut out in the fateful year 1921, Akhmatova polished every line and substituted whole new stanzas. Although the celebrated 'masquerade' about her Petersburg acquaintances in the year 1913 has more the atmosphere of a dance of death than of a carnival, she took great pleasure in reconstructing the vanished world of her youth.

There is a description of Akhmatova from this time by a police informer. I will quote it because it seems to me to have the ring of authenticity, at least to be more scrupulous and to the point than the routine denunciations of later decades. Evidently it wasn't only gastronomy and shoe-cleaning that suffered a qualitative decline under true socialism, but also the art of police informing.

Akhmatova has many acquaintances. She has no close friends. She is good-natured and does not hesitate to spend her money when she has it. But at heart she is cold and arrogant, with a childish egoism. She is help-less when it comes to the practical tasks of everyday life. Mending a stocking poses an insoluble problem for her. Boiling potatoes is an achievement. Despite her great fame she is very shy . . . She tries to keep her nose clean politically, she is proud that Stalin has taken an interest in her. She is Russian to the core. She has never betrayed her feeling for her country. She doesn't go to the publishers with her poems. She hates the Writers' Union

Courtyard of Fountain House, St Petersburg, Akhmatova's home for over twenty years

and considers it a hotbed of sinister intriguers. She can hold her drink – wine as well as vodka.

According to another informer's report, Akhmatova considered the Writers' Union 'an idiotic kindergarten where everyone is punished and has to stand in the corner . . . They print rubbish by Simonov but not Voloshin or Khodasevich or Mandelstam.'

This was the figure whom Isaiah Berlin met in November 1945. 'It was very barely furnished,' he recalls of Akhmatova's room in Fountain House; 'virtually everything in it had, I gathered, been taken away – looted or sold – during the Siege; there was a small table, three or four chairs, a wooden chest, a sofa and, above the unlit stove, a drawing by Modigliani.' In a report for the Foreign Office

Drawing of Akhmatova by Modigliani, 1911

he generalized on these initial impressions: 'The problem
of food and fuel is still fairly acute, and the writers I saw
. . . could not be said to be living with any degree of real
comfort . . .'

In his memoirs *People, Years and Life*, published in Russia
in 1960, Ilya Ehrenburg describes the room in Fountain
House in similar terms:

The room in which Anna Andreyevna Akhmatova lives,
in an old Leningrad house, is small, severe and bare. The
only decoration is a portrait of Akhmatova as a young
woman that hangs on one wall – a drawing by
Modigliani. Anna Andreyevna told me how she had met
the young, extraordinarily shy Italian artist in Paris, who
asked her permission to draw her. That had been in
1911. Akhmatova was not yet Akhmatova, but nor was
Modigliani yet Modigliani.

When Lydia Chukovskaya asked Akhmatova what she thought of Ehrenburg's description, she replied indignantly: 'Not a word of it is true . . . My walls are not bare, and I knew very well who Modigliani was. He lies about everything.' Perhaps this irritation was provoked by Ehrenburg's black and white journalistic style, and above all by his urge to interpret her past. For in her own memoirs Akhmatova confirms the truth of his account of the meeting with Modigliani, and as for his description of the room – as it was at the time – and indeed of Akhmatova's whole milieu, it seems sensitive and tactful in the extreme.

Chukovskaya saw Akhmatova for the first time for many years in 1959, in Leningrad in her flat on Krasnaya Konnitsa, and her account of this visit bears out Ehrenburg's description of Akhmatova's domestic surroundings.

> In the stairwell – darkness and dirt. Akhmatova's stairwell! All this was Akhmatova's – tears came! . . .
>
> I suddenly found myself among long forgotten objects from a distant time: the same frame round the clouded mirror, the same armchair with a broken leg. And the same little mahogany table which had stood twenty years before in the room in Fountain House . . .
>
> Objects suck up time like sponges and pour it over one from head to toe when one comes upon them unexpectedly after long separation. For Anna Akhmatova, the objects in her room were probably full of the year 1913.

Even the Modigliani drawing, the most precious of Akhmatova's possessions, which in later decades was such an attraction for visitors, only underlined the poet's lifelong poverty. Anatoly Nayman tells of a visit paid by an Oxford student to 42 Lenin Street, the third home of the Punin family, where Akhmatova lived in one of its three rooms. They spoke of Modigliani, and the young man asked to see the drawing. Akhmatova took him by the arm and drew him tactfully towards her bed-corner, where the work hung. The guest threw a hurried, embarrassed glance at the portrait and sat down at the table again. Akhmatova commented: 'These young men are not accustomed to looking at old ladies' beds . . . They cannot believe that we live like that. And they cannot imagine that we even write under such conditions.'

A stately, grey-haired lady, a white shawl draped round her shoulders, slowly rose to greet us. Anna Andreyevna Akhmatova was immensely dignified, with unhurried gestures, a noble head, beautiful, somewhat severe features, and an expression of immense sadness. I bowed – it seemed appropriate, for she looked and moved like a tragic queen . . .

Thus Akhmatova appeared to Isaiah Berlin when he first saw her. The scene has all the makings of the most intense kind of theatre. The setting alone, the bleak room with the historic backdrop of the old Sheremetev Palace, was full of promise of emotional or moral events on a grand scale. What took place that night was to be true drama.

But first an incident took place to which both Berlin and Akhmatova were later to attach considerable significance. Randolph Churchill, then a British newpaper correspondent, was staying in Leningrad at the same time as Berlin. When he arrived at his hotel he chanced to hear that Isaiah Berlin, who had been a fellow student at Oxford, was in the city. He went to look for him, eager for companionship and an unofficial interpreter. He found his way to Fountain House and shouted up from the forecourt: 'Isaiah! Isaiah!' This was a highly conspicuous scene for the conditions of the time, full of potential problems and dangers for any Soviet citizen involved. Berlin therefore decided to take temporary leave of Akhmatova, and later phoned to reschedule his visit for nine o'clock that evening.

The drama that we may entitle 'Conversation in Fountain House', which began with Berlin's second arrival, was in three acts. In the first the protagonists were introduced to each other. In this act a third character, an Assyriologist, was also present, a student of Akhmatova's second husband, Vladimir Shileyko. This young woman caused a good deal of tension; being one of those naïve people who never recognize the moment for departure, she stayed until midnight, plying Berlin with a constant stream of questions about 'English universities and their organization'. As Berlin recalls, 'Akhmatova was plainly uninterested and, for the most part, silent.' These first three hours of the twelve-hour meeting, however, were important. For not only did they represent a period of unspoken communication between guest and hostess, but at the same time they created a bond of complicity between them, in their shared desire to be rid of the uninvited and tactless visitor.

The second act lasted a further three hours and consisted of two scenes. One of these was given over to what might be called 'reconnaissance', while the other was alive with emotion. Isaiah Berlin told me how the whole atmosphere changed completely, becoming one of intimate confidentiality, as soon as the door closed behind the young Assyriologist.

First, Akhmatova asked about old friends and acquaintances who had emigrated:

we talked about the composer Artur Lurié, whom I had met in America during the war; he had been an intimate friend of hers and had set some of her and of Mandelstam's poetry to music; about the poet [Georgy] Adamovich; about Boris Anrep, the mosaicist . . . She . . . showed me a ring with a black stone which Anrep had given to her in 1917. She asked after Salome Halpern, *née* Andronikova . . . whom she knew well in St Petersburg before the First World War – a celebrated society beauty of that period . . . Akhmatova told me . . . that Mandelstam, who had been in love with her [Andronikova], dedicated one of his most beautiful poems to her . . . She asked after Vera Stravinsky, the composer's wife, whom I did not then know . . . She spoke of her visits to Paris before the First World War, of her friendship with Amedeo Modigliani, whose drawing of her hung over her fireplace – one of many (the rest had perished during the siege) . . .

In the course of this evocation of the past, Isaiah Berlin played an innocent, passive role. He did not yet know that by answering Akhmatova's questions to the best of his knowledge and belief, he had made himself her companion on a shared journey through time. Akhmatova was moving, as she had done continuously since 1940, on the time-plane of *Poem Without a Hero*. She considered the loss of her pre-revolutionary world to have been the beginning of the unfolding tragedy of her subsequent life. Berlin's answers to her questions, therefore, led inevitably and without transition straight into the second scene – to the first emotional high-point of the meeting.

She spoke . . . of her first husband, the celebrated poet Gumilyov . . . She was convinced that he had not taken part in the monarchist conspiracy for which he had been executed . . . her eyes had tears in them when she described the harrowing circumstances of his death.

Akhmatova showed her tears to very few. Not that she was inhibited about revealing her emotions; her violent outbursts of anger and scorn and her paroxysms of laughter had been witnessed by many. She had little concern for the effect of such reactions on others. She kept herself under strict control in one respect only: on no account would she allow herself to be an object of pity. During this night, however, she was frequently in tears.

> Then she spoke her own poems from *Anno Domini*, *The White Flock*, *From Six Books* . . . She then recited the (at that time) still unfinished *Poem Without a Hero* . . . Even then I realized that I was listening to a work of genius . . .
>
> Then she read the *Requiem*, from a manuscript. She broke off and spoke of the years 1937–8, when both her husband and her son had been arrested and sent to prison camps . . . She spoke in a dry, matter-of-fact voice, occasionally interrupting herself with 'No, I cannot, it is no good, you come from a society of human beings, whereas here we are divided into human beings and – ' Then a long silence. 'And even now – ' I asked about Mandelstam: she was silent, her eyes filled with tears, and she begged me not to speak of him.

Although it was already three in the morning, Berlin records that Akhmatova 'showed no sign of wishing me to leave. I was far too moved and absorbed to stir.' He must by now have realized that Akhmatova was opening herself to him with an extraordinary degree of frankness.

The second act of the nocturnal drama of November 1945 ended in action. 'The door opened and her son Lev Gumilyov entered . . . He seemed cheerful and . . . offered me a dish of boiled potatoes, which was all that they had. Akhmatova apologized for the poverty of her hospitality.'

According to the German translation of Berlin's memoir published in the Munich journal *Transatlantik* in autumn 1983, Akhmatova herself went into the kitchen and came back with a plate of boiled potatoes. There were many inaccuracies in this translation, and, remembering the KGB agent's remark that boiling potatoes was 'an achievement' for Akhmatova, I wondered what the true facts of this particular matter were. If she really had cooked the potatoes, I thought, then this would have been the second emotional climax of the drama, perhaps the prosaic and at the same time ethereal moment of the birth of love.

So I asked Isaiah Berlin in a London café, in the manner of a public prosecutor in search of hard evidence: 'Who boiled the potatoes?' 'She did, naturally,' was the reply. Maybe 'naturally' – but in fact? Berlin, as the guest, had stayed in the living room; he would not have been able to see. Perhaps it had been Irina Punina? Or perhaps one of the men in the communal flat, though this would have been untypical of a Russian household? Here was one of Anna Akhmatova's secrets more precious than any held by the KGB . . .

And while on the subject of this modest nocturnal meal, we must imagine that not only plates but also glasses were surely placed on the little table. Akhmatova writes of 'New Year wine' at the opening of *Poem Without a Hero*, in the context of the meeting with Berlin, but it could equally well have been vodka, which was not hard to come by even in this period of post-war scarcity.

Berlin talked in some detail with Lev Gumilyov, of whom he had a warm and positive impression: 'it was plain that his relation to his mother and hers to him were deeply affectionate'. Akhmatova's son spoke openly about his life; things now seemed to be going well for him; 'he had been allowed to join a prisoners' unit of anti-aircraft gunners and had just returned from Germany. He seemed

cheerful and confident that he could once more live and
work in Leningrad.'

So revealing did Berlin find his conversation with Lev
Gumilyov that he referred to it, without naming names, in
a report he wrote on his trip for the Foreign Office:

> I can say from my personal meetings with one young
> member of the Red Army, lately back from Berlin and
> son of a person liquidated many years ago, that he was
> at least as civilized, well-read, independent, and indeed
> as fastidious, to the point almost of intellectual eccen-
> tricity, as the most admired undergraduate intellectuals
> in Oxford or Cambridge.

The third act of our drama is the least well documented,
and large parts of it are apocryphal. It began at about four
in the morning, when Gumilyov went to his plank-bed in
the small adjoining room, and lasted until nine. Discussion
ranged in depth over Pushkin, Tolstoy, Dostoyevsky,
Turgenev, Chekhov, Pasternak and foreign authors such
as Kafka, Joyce and Eliot as well as personal subjects.
Akhmatova spoke about the principal relationships in her
life – her stimulating but fraught relations with Gumilyov,
the almost unbearable marriage to the insanely jealous
Shileyko, and the complete fiasco with Punin, now sleeping in the next room – all of them important figures but
none of whom could cope with a wife or partner considerably more important than themselves. The name of
Garshin was not mentioned.

We do not know what Berlin told Akhmatova about
himself, and he has the right of silence in the matter. But
that night we may imagine that he too must have opened
his heart and laid aside the mask of the British diplomat,
the style of the promising academic specialist, his young
man's cheerful exterior. The woman before him was inter-

ested only in his innermost being. What remained after removal of the outer layers was the young Jew from Riga who as a child had taken the Russian language with him into exile and had built up around it an education and an understanding of the world that made him an important figure in his new homeland. Only in the light of such considerations could Akhmatova have been so profoundly affected that, in a stanza of *Poem Without a Hero* written down at lightning speed shortly after his departure, she chose him as her 'Guest from the Future'.

This designation, however, is claimed by some contemporaries to have originated earlier. Emma Gerstein, a close friend of Akhmatova from the 1930s onwards, thought it possible that the name might originally have been applied to Dr Garshin, the 'future' in this case being understood as the joint life they planned in Leningrad. When that relationship ended, Akhmatova removed all traces of Garshin from her life, even earlier dedications of poems to him. In the 1990s the Punin family claimed the honour for Anna Akhmatova's long-standing partner, the art historian Nikolay Punin, of being the 'Guest from the Future', and indeed no less than 'addressee and hero of Akhmatova's lyric poetry'.

The growing number of potential 'guests' at Fountain House is somewhat reminiscent of the rivalry between Greek cities for recognition as the birthplace of Homer. On the other hand, the focus of attention on an actual person in this connection impedes understanding of an essentially literary figure. The 'Guest from the Future' is a highly abstract summation of what Berlin's visit symbolized for Akhmatova.

Nadezhda Mandelstam's interpretation would seem the most appropriate: 'The "Guest from the Future" in *Poem* is far from being some cryptic creation such as those that lovers of hidden meanings are so fond of. He is in the first

Isaiah Berlin in the 1950s

place the reader of the future, and secondly a wholly concrete person ... He is a prototype of the reader of the
future, for in that accursed year no one in our country
could read properly.'

This interpretation is remarkable for encompassing not only the 'guest' but also the 'future', a dimension that had played an important part in Russian poetry since the beginning of the twentieth century. Futurists like Mayakovsky, Khlebnikov and Burlyuk had called themselves *budetlyany*, meaning 'citizens of the future'.

Utopians from Campanella to Fourier have located desirable conditions in imaginary countries or cities. Akhmatova too may have expressed in the word 'future' no clearly defined or existing idea of a community, and when tears flowed at the words 'you come from a society of human beings', discovered the island of Utopia before she ever did British shores.

I learned in the course of a long interview with Ramin Jahanbegloo, compiler of an 'intellectual biography in conversations' of Isaiah Berlin, that, although rejecting all forms of communism, he was fascinated by the utopian socialists of the nineteenth century. Before meeting Akhmatova and Pasternak he could scarcely have suspected that he would see citizens of a state created under the sign of Utopia, of all people, finding their virtually unqualified ideal in the free world: 'Both belonged among those,' remembering his most important interlocutors, 'who nourished exaggerated illusions about Western intellectual and artistic culture.'

Illusions can be fatal to politicians, but they do poets no harm. Thus the illusion that Isaiah Berlin was a 'Guest from the Future' proved highly productive for Akhmatova. In this connection Anatoly Nayman has observed: 'The meeting defined . . . her poetic cosmos and had a profound impact on his ideas, mobilizing his creative powers . . .'

And now we come to the question of 'love'.

Love is essentially a fiction, a focus of separate feelings such as tenderness and hate, despair and hope, the urge to possess and to be possessed, pain and pleasure, joy and grief. At the same time it is an independent, self-sufficient reality, the only one apart from birth and death in which human beings can be totally involved. Its erotic components, the act of love itself, embody an urge to exclusivity in which the experience of the lovers is an antipole to the rest of the world.

On the other hand love, even unrequited love, is always a relationship, a continual attempt to pass beyond the boundaries of the ego and of the other person. Anna Akhmatova's response to Isaiah Berlin certainly had this aspect. The diplomat's visit to Fountain House, his arrival and departure, the subjects of conversation, things seen and heard, the smell of his cigar – all this came to shape a kind of prehistory. The poet had to prolong the action, extend the conversation, in order to recall the past. A single meeting and parting are sufficient to maintain the tension of any love story.

The improbability of a further meeting only strengthened the bond that formed the heart of the relationship between Akhmatova and Berlin.

> Thus, torn from the earth,
> We rose up, like stars

wrote Akhmatova, in what was to be the first poem in the cycle *Cinque*, soon after their meeting. One month later, in what was to be the second poem in this sequence, she again placed the memory of that night on a celestial plane:

> That late-night dialogue turned into
> The delicate shimmer of interlaced rainbows.

Even eighteen years later, when the intensity of the original experience must long since have faded, a poem significantly entitled 'The Visit at Night' shows her looking forward to a new, cosmic meeting, this time not on an astral but on a musical plane:

> Not on the leaf-strewn asphalt
>   Will you have to wait.
> But in a Vivaldi adagio
>   We will meet.

It must often have seemed to the poet as though this constructed transcendence was nothing but a consoling falsehood, an astronomical trick:

> This black and everlasting separation
> I bear equally with you.
> Why are you crying? Rather give me your hand,
> Promise to visit my dreams again.
> You and I are like two mountains . . .
> You and I will not meet in this world.
> If only at the midnight hour
> You'd send me a greeting across the stars.

A striking note of hopelessness is struck in this third poem, entitled 'In a Dream', in the cycle *Sweetbrier in Blossom*. Akhmatova first places herself exclusively on an earthly plane, while for all future forms of meeting other planes of 'reality' are constructed – stars, rainbows, music. Secondly, she has her own clear idea of the 'mutuality' of the relationship. She does not grieve over the separation, but gives consolation to her beloved, who must share the burden of love with her. Furthermore, the loved one is no less present than when she first met him:

> Away with time and away with space,
> I descried everything through the white night:

> The narcissus in crystal on your table,
> And the blue smoke of a cigar

In the second poem (written in June 1946) of the
Sweetbrier in Blossom sequence, 'the blue smoke of a cigar'
has concrete meaning, appearing first in the interpolated
stanza to *Poem Without a Hero* that was written so rapidly
after Berlin's visit. And all these 'white nights', 'midnights',
'conversations at night', 'visits at night' are unequivocally
legitimized by that actual magical November night of 1945,
the source of all the emotional energies that the poet has
invested in the maintenance of this metaphysical relationship.

During our conversation in London I asked Isaiah
Berlin, unquestionably the central figure in the last period
of Akhmatova's life, whether he ever had similar feelings
towards her. 'No,' he replied, 'there was no Utopia for me.'
His feelings towards Akhmatova are expressed in terms of
fascination, respect, admiration and sympathy. Later, he
was unable to exclude the possibility that he had at least a
part share in causing her persecution, and guilt feelings
became dominant.

What, however, appears to have been the nature of
Akhmatova's emotions as she experienced them in the
untroubled first phase of her love? At this point the truly
dramatic existed only in vague premonitions. What was it
that moved her, in what place was she struck by Cupid's
arrow? In the third poem in the cycle *Cinque*, written on
20 December 1945, she confesses with extraordinary
openness:

> For so long I hated
> To be pitied,
> But one drop of your pity
> And I go around as if the sun were in my body.

> That's why there is dawn all around me.
> I go around creating miracles,
> That's why!

Only one interpretation of this seems possible. The impact made by the nocturnal visitor had succeeded in breaking down his hostess's natural reserve. She was thus able to reveal the tragic content of her life to a stranger. There are bashful indications in Berlin's memoir that her confession was not restricted to the politically caused problems of her life:

> As the night wore on, Akhmatova grew more and more animated. She questioned me about my personal life. I answered fully and freely, as if she had an absolute right to know ... Our conversation, which touched on intimate details of both her life and my own, wandered from literature and art, and lasted until ... the morning of the following day.

Akhmatova's comparison of the 'Guest from the Future' with Virgil's Aeneas led a number of her contemporaries to interpret the nocturnal meeting as a classical allusion, a modern version of the episode of Dido and Aeneas: the Carthaginian queen, listening to Aeneas's tale of the fall of Troy, is overcome with pity and falls in love with her guest, who, however, grows weary of her hospitality and steals away with his fleet, whereupon Dido, her passion thwarted, ends her life on a pyre.

Many atmospheric elements of this epic story may be seen to have parallels in the nocturnal meeting in Leningrad; nevertheless, the latter is diametrically opposed to the Latin model. In Fountain House it is not the guest but the hostess who tells the story, not the man but the woman. The outcome of the meeting, despite all its problematic consequences, is not the flaming pyre but a tragic feeling of joy. The British scholar was the first man to whom Anna Akhmatova uninhibitedly showed her weakness, her vulnerability – at a critical moment of her life, on the threshold of age and isolation. Here, then, was an act of liberation in the middle of its very opposite:

> Neither despair, nor shame,
> Not now, not after, not then.

These lines were written shortly after Berlin's visit to Fountain House. Akhmatova's meeting with him has prompted another parallel – Joseph Brodsky has spoken in terms of Romeo and Juliet. But this is not a true parallel. Shakespeare's lovers miss happiness by a hair's-breadth: had Friar Laurence come to the churchyard sooner, he would have averted the tragedy. The Leningrad story, by contrast, left no room for chance. Catastrophe did not hang over Fountain House, it was in the house itself.

The relationship offers a model of its own, which may also be taken as classic. In Leningrad the two protagonists have the opportunity to re-establish the temporal and spatial continuity of the world, broken off in 1913. In taking this opportunity they bring upon themselves the anger of the cosmic powers. The world is and remains as it was – split, and the attempt to overcome the isolation of its two separate halves through love is doomed to failure. Akhmatova is aware of this, but has no means of avoiding failure. To quote the last poem once more:

> And that door that you half opened
> I don't have the strength to slam.

She even suspects that she and Berlin have split the world still further; we shall return to this.

'I go around creating miracles' essentially means: 'I write poems.' And these poems are the only evidence of any substance about Akhmatova's continuing 'love' for Isaiah Berlin. In spring 1946 Akhmatova visited her friend the actress Nina Ardova in Moscow. They talked of the past, of the war and Akhmatova's future plans, of her son Lev who had returned from the army to Leningrad in the autumn and now lived with her. 'Then she began to talk of something else,' Ardova reports, 'a meeting with someone who had a place in her lyric poetry for many years after that, beginning with the *Cinque* cycle.'

On her return from Moscow Akhmatova sent Ardova all the Berlin poems with the dedication: 'In memory of all our night-time conversations'. She wrote down the famous addition to *Poem Without a Hero* in first draft:

> *The guest from the future! Is it possible?*
> *Scarcely four weeks will go by*
> *And darkness will send him to me.*

In the final draft she was to reformulate these lines, making them historically specific:

> *The guest from the future! – Is it true*
> *That he really will come to me,*
> *Turning left at the bridge?*

Akhmatova presented the *Cinque* cycle at a private reading in Moscow, with the poet Boris Slutsky and the pianist Svyatoslav Richter present. The poems had already been published in the journal *Leningrad*, with the awkward title, in Italian and in Latin script, altered to: *Five Poems from the cycle 'Love'*.

'I go around creating miracles' – not only did Akhmatova create miracles, but miracles happened to her. In spring

1946 she had a successful season. In Moscow and Leningrad she took part in many readings. Everywhere, wearing her black dress and wrapped in a white shawl, she was enthusiastically received.

Nina Ardova was present in the Hall of Columns in Moscow's House of Unions on 3 April 1946 when Akhmatova was asked by the public to read from her published volumes. 'People called out [the titles of her best known poems]. She would make a gesture of refusal, frown, and then give a sly smile.' Another witness, Natalya Roskina, describes how Akhmatova even had to protect herself from the enthusiasm of the public. 'When the public asked to hear more poems, she would say: "I don't know my poems by heart, and I haven't brought any more." The public understood that she could not say otherwise. The applause thundered on.'

Akhmatova stood on the eve of a new triumph so far unprecedented in her life. Two volumes of her poetry, one case-bound and one in paperback, were about to be published. Barring the unforeseen, her literary resurrection was to take place that summer.

In diplomatic terms, Berlin was highly satisfied with his visit to Leningrad:

> life seems politically easier . . . than in Moscow . . . The writers . . . actors in the theatres . . . assistants in the bookshops . . . as well as passengers in trams and buses seem slightly better bred and educated than their cosier but more primitive counterparts in Moscow . . . I found no trace of that xenophobia in Leningrad, signs of which are discernible in the minds of some of even the most enlightened intellectuals in Moscow . . .

He concluded optimistically that it might be a good idea to open a consulate in Leningrad. It was typical of this optimistic period shortly before the outbreak of the Cold War that the British ambassador in Moscow, Frank Roberts, forwarded the idea to the Foreign Minister, Ernest Bevin.

At the same time, Berlin was not to be taken in; he was aware of the insecurity of the post-war situation. 'Present freedom of circulation [in Leningrad],' he wrote, 'may well be due to the absence of resident representatives of foreign institutions and countries which makes the task of sur- veillance . . . relatively easier.' He also noticed the social difference between privileged writers and others: 'the difference between Communists and non-Communists was . . . pretty well marked. The main advantage of belonging to the Party was the better material conditions . . . but the main disadvantage consisted in the duty of grinding out a great deal of lifeless government propa- ganda at frequent intervals and of appalling length . . . '

In general Berlin was sceptical about the outlook for writers in the Soviet Union, and well aware of the situ- ation regarding contact with foreigners. 'Over the entire scene of Russian literature,' he wrote in a second despatch to the Foreign Office,

> there broods a curious air of stillness, with not a breath of wind. It may be that this is the calm before the next great tidal wave . . .
>
> Writers, who are generally considered as persons who need a good deal of watching, since they deal in the dangerous commodity of ideas, are fended off from private, individual contact with foreigners with greater care than the less intellectual professionals, such as actors, dancers and musicians, who are regarded as less susceptible to the power of ideas, and to that extent better insulated against disturbing influences from abroad . . . Known contact with foreigners does not, of

course, necessarily lead to disgrace or persecution, but the more timorous among the writers, and particularly those who have not thoroughly secured their position and become the mouthpiece of the Party line, avoid discoverable meetings with foreigners – even amongst the Communists and fellow-travellers of proven loyalty who arrive on official Soviet-sponsored visits.

Berlin sensed, however, a rather special international mood among Leningrad writers.

They hoped . . . that as Leningrad developed into a port communicating with the outside world more information and perhaps more foreigners would begin to visit their city and so bring them in touch with the world, isolation from which they appear to feel very deeply. My own visits, though arranged quite openly through one of my bookshop acquaintances, had been the first, literally the first I was told, made by any foreigner since 1917 . . .

Berlin had frank literary discussions: 'I obtained the general impression that there are few real illusions about the actual quality of the work of Soviet writers . . . Thus everyone seemed to take it for granted that Boris Pasternak was a poet of genius and that Simonov was a glib journalist and little more.'

Despite his general scepticism, then, some of the belief in relative liberalization held by many Russian intellectuals after the war rubbed off on Berlin. On his return to Oxford to resume his academic career, he embarked on a hazardous project: the attempt to secure the award of an honorary doctorate of literature to Boris Pasternak, together with an invitation to him to come to Oxford to receive it. This noble-minded scheme, doomed to failure at the outset, may be reconstructed from the reply received by Berlin from the Vice-Chancellor of Oxford University, Richard Livingstone, dated 1 June 1946. The Vice-Chancellor is clearly concerned to dissuade his young colleague from his rash plan:

> In spite of your most persuasive letter I remain a heretic. I do not much like the use of Honorary Degrees for political purposes (though obviously Pasternak has other claims), nor do I feel that this is the moment for a 'gesture' to Russia. However, if Bowra cares to raise the question in Council, that would test the opinion of this body. It seems in any case that Pasternak's visit to England is very uncertain, and as you say August is not an ideal moment for a Degree ceremony.

Remembering the disaster of the award of the Nobel Prize to Pasternak some years later, we can be grateful to the Vice-Chancellor that he did not agree to an invitation that, with hindsight, we can now see would have been dangerous to the poet. On the other hand, it is good that Isaiah Berlin brought his idea from Moscow to Oxford and eventually carried it through, even if the process took nearly two decades and Pasternak was no longer alive to witness it.

On the point of leaving the Soviet Union via Finland at the beginning of January 1946, Berlin made a short stop in Leningrad during which he paid another visit to Akhmatova to say good-bye. About this presumably fleeting second visit very little is known. Berlin mentions it in a letter to the British ambassador in Moscow in which he comments that his second visit to Leningrad had been diplomatically uneventful, though he had seen again 'the poetess . . . who finally inscribed a brand new poem about

6 January 1946, the day after Berlin's second, farewell visit

midnight conversations for my benefit, which is the most thrilling thing that has ever, I think, happened to me'. The poem was one of the first three of the great cycle *Cinque*, the most immediate literary result of the encounter.

Back in Oxford, Berlin received a letter from Boris Pasternak dated 26 June 1946, the poet taking on the exotic role of *postillon d'amour*. 'When Akhmatova was here,' he wrote,

her every third word was – you. And so dramatically and mysteriously! At night, for example, in a taxi on the way back from some evening or reception, inspired and weary, and slightly in the clouds, in French: Notre ami (that's you) a dit . . . , or a promis etc. etc. In the end, those of her friends who were jealous of her [attach-ment] to you began to pester me with requests: B[oris] L[eonidovich], please describe Berlin for us, who is he and what is he like? Then followed my praises, and only then did their [real] torments begin. Everyone loves you and recalls you with great warmth.

When this letter was written, Anna Akhmatova must have been walking the streets of Leningrad 'as if the sun were in her body', ready to 'go around creating miracles'. The authorities decreed otherwise. Shortly after Berlin's second, good-bye visit in January, her room was bugged and all the informers in her neighbourhood were ordered to redouble their efforts. In her memoirs Nadezhda Mandelstam states her opinion that Akhmatova was under surveillance from this time onward.

2 *Excommunication*

On the evening of 7 August 1946 Anna Akhmatova took the stage of the Bolshoy Dramatic Theatre in Leningrad. The city was commemorating the twenty-fifth anniversary of the death of Aleksandr Blok. Akhmatova's appearance was a direct continuation of her highly successful Moscow readings. 'When she appeared on the stage,' recalls Dmitry Maksimov, historian of Russian poetry, 'the whole audience rose to its feet with passionate applause that went on and on . . . She began to read, and many, with half-closed eyes, murmured the lines with her, which they knew by heart':

> I visited the poet.
> Precisely at noon. Sunday.
> It was quiet in the spacious room,
> And beyond the windows, intense cold
>
> And a raspberry sun
> Above shaggy, bluish smoke . . .
> How keenly my taciturn host
> Regarded me!
>
> He had the kind of eyes
> That everyone must recall,
> It was better for me to be careful,
> And not look at them at all . . .

What accounted for the fascination of poems like this? Perhaps more than literary quality it was their subject-matter and their individuality that attracted the audience.

Russian poetry-lovers were not exactly spoilt at this time. In the 1940s lyric poets were mouthpieces for a state that behaved as if it were sole repository of all values. Nine out of ten poems were about the war; Aleksey Surkov's 'Song of the Brave' is representative:

> Threatening clouds pile up,
> The air is lit by flashes,
> Dust-clouds whirl, through it all
> The trumpets sound the alarm.
> Death to Fascism! The soviet
> Calls the brave to battle.
> The bullet fears the brave,
> The bayonet the courageous.

The 'brave' and 'courageous' were sick and tired of dithyrambs of this kind. In Leningrad above all, with its half a million dead in the Siege, there was a kind of psychological vitamin starvation after the war, a longing for basic intimate emotion, even if only in poetry. Anna Akhmatova's poem in homage to Blok, written in January 1914, radiated the warmth and melancholy of a healthy world, now lost, whose last representative was Akhmatova herself.

'This was an encounter,' continues Maksimov, 'with a half-forgotten, newly discovered poet.' For most of the audience that evening, it was their last encounter with Anna Akhmatova. Her next public reading was not to be for twenty years.

On that very evening two leading cultural officials, Georgy Aleksandrov and Aleksandr Yegolin, sent a working paper entitled 'On the unsatisfactory situation regarding the journals *Zvezda* and *Leningrad*' to Andrey Zhdanov, Secretary of the Central Committee of the Party and Stalin's cultural watchdog. The paper criticized numerous Leningrad writers including Mikhail Zoshchenko and

Anna Akhmatova, the latter being far from the chief target. The Leningrad party leaders, members of the executive committee of the city's branch of the Writers' Union and the editors of the two journals under attack were summoned urgently to Moscow for a meeting on 9 August. At the organizational headquarters of the Party a meeting took place in which Stalin, together with other members of the Politburo, was personally involved. A document was being prepared which saw the light of day on 14 August as the Central Committee's Resolution *On the Journals 'Zvezda' and 'Leningrad'*. It was Zhdanov's task to explain the draft content of this document to the Leningrad intellectuals.

Over the next week cultural officials distributed to writers, artists and Leningrad editors invitations to an 'important' meeting to be held at the Leningrad branch of the Union of Writers. No one was told what the event was to be about. Mikhail Zoshchenko, officially still a member of the editorial board of *Zvezda*, asked for an entrance ticket. However, he was prevented from attending on various pretexts. The meeting between Leningrad intellectuals and the leaders of the Party therefore took place on 16 August without him.

At 5 p.m. precisely Andrey Zhdanov entered the Great Hall of the Smolny Institute, where Lenin had announced the Soviet takeover of power. He took the chair, surrounded by prominent writers and literary functionaries. 'We felt exceedingly apprehensive from the very first moments in the Smolny Institute,' recalls one eyewitness, who even in 1977, publishing his reminiscences in a Russian émigré journal, preferred to use the initials 'D.D.' instead of his own name.

> The historic premises, the threefold entry check, the large number of invited writers, journalists, and film, broadcasting and publishing personnel, the whole

atmosphere of strict ceremonial, made the occasion something far more than an everyday meeting . . . The hall was mute, rigid, ice-cool, and in the course of those three hours seemed transformed into a piece of hard white stone. One writer was suddenly taken ill and staggered towards the exit, which was barred by armed soldiers. The meeting, including sycophantic contributions from the floor and hysterical self-criticism from writers taking part, lasted almost until midnight. Eventually, several hundred people slowly and silently left the building, and walked equally silently along the long, straight alley to the next square to take the last buses and trolleybuses home.

The central part of Zhdanov's speech was as follows:

I come now to the question of Anna Akhmatova's literary work. Her verse has recently appeared in Leningrad journals in print runs of increased size. Anna Akhmatova is one of the representatives of a reactionary literary quagmire devoid of ideas. She belongs to the literary group of the so-called Acmeists, which emerged at one time out of the ranks of the Symbolists, and is one of the standard-bearers of a hollow, empty, aristocratic-salon poetry, which is absolutely foreign to Soviet literature . . .

Anna Akhmatova's subject-matter is thoroughly individualistic. The range of her poetry is pitifully limited – this is the poetry of a feral lady from the salons, moving between the boudoir and the prayer-stool. It is based on erotic motifs linked with motifs of mourning, melancholy, death, mysticism and isolation. The feeling of isolation, an understandable feeling for the social consciousness of a group that is dying out, the gloomy, hopeless notes of the dying, mystic experiences intermingled with eroticism – this is the spiritual world of

Akhmatova, a fragment from the ruins of the irretrievable world of the old aristocratic culture, the 'good old days of Catherine', now vanished for ever. She is half nun, half whore, or rather both whore and nun, fornication and prayer being intermingled in her world ... Such is Anna Akhmatova, with her petty, narrow private life, her trivial experiences and her religious-mystical eroticism. Akhmatova's poetry is totally foreign to the people.

At this point, towards the end of the first hour of his speech, Zhdanov already had Mikhail Zoshchenko lined up in his sights as an 'un-Soviet writer', a 'hypocrite', a 'tasteless petty bourgeois', a 'rogue' and even a 'deserter' (during the Siege of Leningrad). In the smear campaign that followed his speech Akhmatova was not spared the infamous charge of desertion either. The documentary evidence is quite clear that at the beginning of the Siege Zoshchenko and Akhmatova had both been evacuated from the city by order of the Central Committee.

Zoshchenko's case concerned a story reprinted in *Zvezda* (no. 1, 1946) after it had first been published in the children's magazine *Mursilka*. Were it not for the story's publishing history and its humorous tone, it might have been possible to summon up a certain sympathy with the Party's case. *The Adventures of a Monkey* is a grotesque portrayal of post-war everyday life in Leningrad seen through the eyes of a monkey escaped from a zoo. Zoshchenko's send-up of official sentiment and ideological language had already got on the nerves of the journal's professional readership, which was ready to react to any new work by Zoshchenko with self-righteous indignation. The reprinting of the story in *Zvezda* was just what these readers had been waiting for, a perfect opportunity to settle old scores with the writer they loved to hate.

Zoshchenko's tragedy lay in the nature of his talents. The protagonists of his best stories of the 1920s and 1930s were figures from the Soviet petite bourgeoisie, and the substance of his satire was the way in which this prolific species incorporated the official language of the time into its everyday idiom. His opponents therefore condemned Zoshchenko as a petit bourgeois writer, while he in turn attempted to answer this rhetoric with the equally unjustified claim that he was simply a critic of the Soviet petite bourgeoisie. In reality his criticism went a good deal further – he was unmasking the mendacious clichés of ideology on a semantic level.

The little man parrots the Soviet view of history:

I have always sympathized with the central convictions. Not once did I ever protest in the era of War Communism when they were bringing in the NEP. If you've got to have the NEP then you've got to have it. I can tell you that. And then, under War Communism, how free things were, as far as culture and civilization, I mean. I mean to say, at the theatre you didn't have to change – just sit in what you came in. Now that was a real achievement.

Or the foreigner seen through the eyes of *homo sovieticus*:

I can always tell a foreigner from a Soviet person. These bourgeois foreigners have something different about their faces. Their faces look, how to say, more rigid, more contemptuous than ours. Anyone who has an expression like that on his face, I mean to say, then he looks at everything with that expression on his face.

And finally, an extract from a speech by the chairman of a housing co-operative to mark the hundredth anniversary of the day of Pushkin's death:

I come now to my conclusion, comrades. Pushkin's influence on us all is enormous. He was a great writer, a writer of genius. One might regret that he didn't live in our own time. We'd have lavished every kind of care and attention on him and made sure that he had a fabulous life – of course, only if we'd known that he was really going to be a Pushkin. It can happen, you know, that someone's contemporaries have hopes of him, they give him a decent life, cars and flats, and after all that it turns out he's neither fish, flesh nor fowl. You can't get anything out of him, as they say. All in all, it's a shady business, being a poet . . . You get much more out of singers. They sing, and you see at once what sort of voice they've got.

Zoshchenko wrote this culturally hostile monologue, with its mildly fascist overtones, in 1937, when he still belonged to the privileged category; it is easy to imagine what he expected as the reverse side of 'every kind of care and attention'. He could only hope that the subversive potential of such quasi-quotations of Soviet everyday utterance might remain unnoticed by the censor. It seems extraordinary that the name of Zoshchenko does not appear in the secret files of senior Party and censorship authorities until 1943.

But what texts could seriously be held against Anna Akhmatova? Zhdanov's speech contains four lines of direct quotation; three poems are referred to directly and a fourth indirectly.

From a Communist viewpoint, poetry in which Akhmatova remembers pre-revolutionary St Petersburg could be imagined to be the most suitable target for criticism. Zhdanov quotes only a single line of this kind: 'Everything is plundered, sold and betrayed . . . ' This line, however, comes from a poem written and published in 1921. Even at that time Proletkult critics had charged

Akhmatova with 'counter-revolutionary sentiments'. On 4 July 1922 one reviewer, Nikolay Osinsky, who had taken an active part in the October Revolution, had protested against these accusations in the chief Party organ *Pravda*, and had not been afraid to write: 'In the chaos of the Revolution much was indeed "plundered, sold and betrayed".' This was a fact that many Communists of that time could live with.

Zhdanov also took offence at a poem published in *Leningrad* 'in which Akhmatova depicts her lonely life [in Tashkent], which she was driven to sharing with a black cat'. The Soviet cultural chief went on to point out suspiciously: 'This subject is not a new one. Akhmatova also wrote about a black cat in 1909.' His assertion that such a feeling of loneliness during the Great War of the Fatherland was illegitimate must have sounded odd even to his audience in 1946.

Zhdanov was seized with fury when he quoted from the collection *Anno Domini*:

> And I swear to you by the garden of the angels,
> I swear by the miracle-working ikon,
> And by the fire and smoke of our nights . . .

Cleverly the chief ideologue, in his holy rage, forgot to mention the substance of this oath: 'I will never come back to you.' He was obsessed with unmasking the poem's religious imagery. These lines read quite differently in the otherwise slavishly exact text of Zhdanov's speech published in the German Democratic Republic:

> . . . before you, angels' [/English] garden
> I bow.
> Bow before the miraculous icon
> And the offspring of our hot nights . . .

This obscene adaptation – with the conscious double meaning of the German word *englisch* – was presumably intended to convey Akhmatova's self-prostration before British imperialism.

Of course, Zhdanov did not give or remind his audience of the date of these lines – they had been written, again, in 1921 and published in 1922, and so had nothing whatsoever to do with the Leningrad journals that were the subject of his criticism. And yet the whole virulent personal attack on Akhmatova, especially the insult 'whore', grew out of these three lines. It is abundantly clear that Zhdanov's diatribe was aimed at the poet personally rather than her poetry.

Now it must be pointed out, for a full appreciation of the facts, that Zhdanov based his denigration of Akhmatova on an authoritative source. In 1922 the important literary critic Boris Eikhenbaum, in one of the first books on Akhmatova, analysed the link between the mystic-religious and the erotic elements in Akhmatova's verse and drew the following conclusion: 'Here already we can see the beginnings of the paradoxical, or more correctly, contradictory, double image of the heroine – half "whore" burning with passion, half "nun" able to pray to God for forgiveness.'

To any experienced reader it should be quite clear that Eikhenbaum is referring here to the 'heroine', the poet's literary persona. The difference between a real-life person and a poetic portrayal of that person is the difference between fact and fiction, dream and reality. When Zhdanov – whether with malicious intent or out of sheer ignorance – identified the poet's lyrical persona with the poet's real-life person, then the word he used, *bludnitsa*, with its biblical overtones of 'loose woman', 'sinner', took on a coarser meaning. Pronounced pointedly by a male tongue, it approximated to the obscene sense of the modern big city term *blyad'*, 'whore'. Zhdanov here drew on the most primitive sexist mass instincts of a society riddled with secret reserves of erotic taboos. Because, in the public mind, Zhdanov's speech and the Central Committee Resolution were one and the same, the double insult 'nun–whore' was elevated to the status of an officially confirmed 'characterization' of the poet. Anna Akhmatova was, so to speak, *appointed* a 'nun and a whore'.

Things went no better for her where the concept of 'eroticism' was concerned. For Eikhenbaum this word belonged to the normal vocabulary of any educated person. The Soviet period brought an abrupt end to neutral vocabulary. Reference works took on an official ideological tone. The entry in the *New Soviet Encyclopedia* on 'eroticism' reads eerily as if the editors of 1935 already had Zhdanov's speech and his characterization of Akhmatova at the back of their minds: 'In classes that are in the process of disintegration . . . eroticism has the character of refined perversion . . . is often linked with mysticism . . . and serves the purposes of flight from reality.' A later edition of the indispensable reference work, that of 1957, is even more succinct and less favourable to Akhmatova: 'Eroticism in art is open, often coarse portrayal of love and sexual life.'

Shortly before her death Anna Akhmatova maintained that she had 'never written an erotic line'. This statement, which, fortunately for world literature, is not a true one, was simply a gesture of self-defence against the official charge of obscenity.

The Russian public did not know at the time that the Central Committee Resolution of 1946, as far as it concerned Akhmatova, had a fairly extended prelude, if not a full-scale dress-rehearsal. This emerges conclusively from secret files in the Agitation and Propaganda Department of the Central Committee of the Soviet Communist Party.

When in the summer of 1940 Akhmatova, after an interval of nineteen years, published her selection *From Six Books*, she found herself in a situation that in many respects anticipated her short-lived post-war fame. At the beginning of the year she had been admitted to membership of the Writers' Union, and such prominent Soviet authors as Aleksey Tolstoy and Aleksandr Fadeyev proposed her for the Stalin Prize. Pasternak was at this time even of the opinion that Akhmatova's new privileges, which could not have been granted without Stalin's knowledge, might help towards Lev Gumilyov's release from camp.

It was not long, however, before it was decided at a higher level that too much fuss was being made of Akhmatova. At the end of September 1940 an employee of the Central Committee, Krupin by name, sent an extremely tendentious selection from her new volume to Zhdanov with the comment: 'The rubbish that Akhmatova writes can be traced to two sources, which are what all her "poetry" is about: God and "free" love. Her "poetic" images on this are borrowed from religious literature.' There followed three pages of quotations seeking to illustrate this theme, including the lines from the cycle *Anno Domini* that Zhdanov was to quote six years later at the Smolny. For the moment, however, he contented himself with marginal comments on Krupin's memo, which he sent on to the head of the Department of Agitation and Propaganda. What he wrote was revealing:

It really is a disgrace that books of verse like this are allowed to be published. How could this 'lechery alongside prayer to the glory of God' ever have seen the light of day? Who supported it? And what is the attitude of Glavlit [the highest censorship authority] towards it? Please clarify and make proposals.

Comrades Aleksandrov and Polikarpov drafted the appropriate resolution and the rest of the edition of *From Six Books* was quietly withdrawn from circulation.

To the end of her life Anna Akhmatova was firmly convinced that the Central Committee Resolution of 14 August 1946, Zhdanov's attack on her, her expulsion from the Writers' Union, and the arrests of Punin and Lev Gumilyov at the end of 1949 were in the main traceable to one and the same cause: all the fateful events of these years were the consequences of Isaiah Berlin's visit to Fountain House. During her stay in Oxford in June 1965 she even maintained to Berlin that their nocturnal conversation in November 1945 had unleashed Stalin's anger and started the Cold War.

Isaiah Berlin has commented on these views of Akhmatova's in memoirs and personal conversation. I detect the sceptical head-shaking of the rationalist:

> She meant it exactly as she said it, and insisted on the truth of her thesis. She considered us both to be figures of world history, appointed by destiny to play a fateful role in a cosmic conflict – and this is reflected in her poems dating from that time. The idea was a major component of her historical-philosophical view of the world, and much of her poetry rested on it.

Indeed, Akhmatova seemed to have no doubts about the significance for world history of her meeting with the 'Guest from the Future'. In the 'Third and Last' Dedication to *Poem Without a Hero* she makes a clear statement:

> Long enough I have frozen in fear,
>   Better to summon a Bach chaconne,
>   And behind it will enter a man,
> He will not be a beloved husband to me
>   But what we accomplish, he and I,
>   Will disturb the Twentieth Century.

The historian in me vigorously opposes the absurd notion that a relationship of this kind could possibly have any effect on conflict or tension between two superpowers. At the same time, however, I sense something suspicious in this rejection, namely the arrogance of the young marxist fatalist who in his heyday would have nothing to do – Get thee behind me, Satan! – with any insufficiently historical-materialist explanation of the world. Such an attitude sprang from the assumption that one held certain marxist theses – like the theory of impoverishment in the development of capitalist countries or that of the gradual withering away of the state in the course of socialist development – to be inalienable, like articles of religious faith. Today none of these axioms seems to me any more rational than, say, belief in a fire-god.

Akhmatova's certainty, however, that her nocturnal conversation with Berlin in Fountain House unleashed the Cold War was rooted in the mindset of her time. The meeting between this celebrated poet and a Western diplomat at a time of growing tensions between the Allied Powers was an act dense with symbolism and therefore a political event of the first importance in the Soviet Union. The spectacle of a First Secretary at the British Embassy walking openly about Leningrad with Randolph Churchill, the son of Stalin's arch-rival, was calculated to put the Kremlin on red alert.

The true danger potential of such a conversation bore no relation to the threat that was seen in it, and nor did its content, even if it could have been known to the authorities in its entirety. In late summer and autumn 1945 Pasternak had weekly meetings with Isaiah Berlin, discussing no less a subject than his half-completed *Doctor Zhivago* with him – and remained wholly unmolested. Some arbitrary or chance factor could have played a part here, some favourable disposition at the highest level of decision-making.

The Stalinist system was no modern institutionalized dictatorship, but an archaic despotism in which the ruler's benevolence or anger was transmitted and realized in action by tens of thousands of functionaries. Whether any particular decision was influenced by toothache, alcohol or anything else was not important, but rather the fact that no social or political force existed that could oppose the will of the dictator. We can no longer trace today whether Stalin's anger over Akhmatova's contact with Berlin really did have a negative effect on Soviet-British relations. But if Stalin had hit on the idea of using the meeting that took place in Fountain House as a pretext for instituting a freeze in these relations, there was no one to stop him in the process. This was understood by Anna Akhmatova but not by Western observers, including Isaiah Berlin, to whom the suggestion occasioned nothing but a politely sceptical smile.

A connection between the meeting and Akhmatova's fall from grace soon afterwards, however, seems clear. The received version of events is that after Berlin's visit to Fountain House, Zhdanov sent 'The Head of the Family', as Stalin was called by his closest subordinates, a detailed report, to which Stalin is supposed to have responded: 'So our nun has been receiving British spies', and then cursed so obscenely that twenty years later Anna Akhmatova was embarrassed to repeat his alleged words to Berlin.

The words 'So our nun has been receiving British spies' are not, in the nature of things, on record. The remark belongs to the legendary store of enquiries about the poet that Stalin is often reputed to have made. In oral tradition the first sentence of such enquiries, repeated in an exaggerated Georgian accent for greater authenticity, was always: 'What's our nun up to?' (*'Chto delayet nasha monakhinya?'*)

Another legend has it that Stalin's anger with Akhmatova was due to her growing popularity. Her Moscow triumph had quickly reached his ears. Nika Glen, Nina Ardova and Lev Gornung all testify that her appearance on the stage was greeted by a standing ovation lasting ten to fifteen minutes. When Zhdanov reported the occasion to Stalin, the Head of the Family is said to have asked: 'Who organized the standing?' Nadezhda Mandelstam cites Zoshchenko as her source for the anecdote and adds: 'In my opinion these words are "not safe to quote", as Pasternak used to say, in other words, they are words that come out of the general lexicon of the person to whom they are attributed.'

It may not have been Stalin's wounded vanity alone, however, that played a part in events, but certain considerations of prestige that were part of the system. There was a strictly regulated hierarchy of applause at public meetings in the Soviet Union: applause, tumultuous applause, prolonged and tumultuous applause, tumultuous applause with the audience half-rising from their seats, and the high-point of all, wild tumultuous applause that went on without end, eventually turning into a standing ovation. Furthermore, it was clearly and individually laid down who was entitled to each of these degrees of applause. At political meetings during the 1950s teams of applause-leaders often stood in readiness, performing their task at a sign from the chair. This was commonly known as 'guided spontaneity'.

At poetry-readings which she had presented in April

Anna Akhmatova and Boris Pasternak, 1946

1946 at the Polytechnic Museum and in the Hall of Columns in the House of Unions, Moscow, Akhmatova had leaped up all the steps of the hierarchy of applause to the very summit. Her own reaction was one of extreme suspicion. 'The prophetically inclined, far from politically naïve Akhmatova,' Natalya Roskina recalls, 'felt at once that this enthusiasm boded no good.' And indeed, these April evenings in 1946 were soon to prove fateful for her. She later remarked of a photograph taken of her and Boris Pasternak at the Writers Club at this time: 'Here I am earning the Central Committee Resolution.'

In using the words 'legend' and 'legendary' I certainly do not have 'untruth' in mind. Under the conditions of an extremely strict censorship many facts, as Isaiah Berlin has said, survive in oral tradition only. The famous telephone conversations between Stalin and Bulgakov or Stalin and Pasternak are important and incontrovertible facts of Russian literary history. For decades, however, they existed only at the level of folklore, were in no way verifiable, and their outline, even their content altered from speaker to speaker. Their common inalienable truth, however, was grounded in the almost intimate relationship that exists between the holders of power in the Soviet Union and writers (if not always literature as such), a relationship of which it has now become possible to offer documentary proof.

Thus in his lecture in Moscow in April 1993 Oleg Kalugin confirmed that after Berlin's visit Akhmatova's flat in Fountain House had been bugged and a number of informers placed close to her. The fact is that the British diplomat was almost automatically classified as a spy, and Akhmatova, as we also know from Kalugin, fell under the same suspicion. There is proof enough that in the Soviet Union at this time literature as well as espionage came within the competence of the highest echelons of power as a 'political problem'. It should therefore be no cause for wonder that the head of state was ready to chat with the next most important figure in the government about the 'petty, narrow private life' of an ageing poet.

Stalin's special interest in Akhmatova's case is shown by the minutes of a meeting of the Organization Bureau which dealt with the 'refractory' Leningrad journals.

Prokofiev [*chairman of the Leningrad Union of Writers*]: As far as the poems are concerned, I don't think it's such a great sin to have published Anna Akhmatova's poems. She is a poet with a quiet voice, and it's normal even for Soviet people to express sadness.

Stalin: Apart from the fact that Anna Akhmatova has a name that has been well-known for some time, what else is there to see in her?

Prokofiev: There are some good poems in her post-war work . . .

Stalin: You can count them on the fingers of one hand.
Prokofiev: She doesn't write many poems on present-day subjects, Josef Vissarionovich. She is a poet of the old school, with fixed views, and so cannot offer anything new.
Stalin: Then she should be published elsewhere. Why in *Zvezda*?
Prokofiev: I have to say that what we've rejected for *Zvezda* has later been printed by *Znamya* [published in Moscow].
Stalin: We'll sort *Znamya* out too. We'll sort them all out.
Prokofiev: Yes, that will be excellent.

The chairman of the Leningrad Union of Writers was clearly trying to persuade Stalin that it would be inappropriate to direct any of the harsh measures of the coming showdown with the two journals against Anna Akhmatova herself. He was trying to convey to the dictator that the Party could not win any propaganda points with an anti-Akhmatova campaign – that the chosen target was too old, weak and harmless. Stalin allowed all these arguments to bounce off him. With childish obstinacy, he was determined to push through Akhmatova's excommunication at any price, as if he wanted to punish her for some specific reason, regardless of all considerations of political advantage and independently of the fate of the two journals.

There was another, perhaps more significant strand to Stalin's motivation: the young Soso Djugashvili had a poetic streak and wrote verse. As soon as he came into contact with a marxist circle in Tiflis, however, and published his first fulminating articles in the Georgian social-democratic journal *Akhali Tskhovreba* (*New Life*), he turned his back on the nobler literary form. Literary authorities of the time, however, noticed his first verse, and a romantic

poem-cycle written when he was eighteen – on his love of
the Caucasian mountains and freedom – found its way into
a representative anthology.

Stalin was not without a certain cultivated literary
taste. Walt Whitman is known to have been his favourite poet, which may be some explanation for his enthusiastic espousal of the avant-garde, activist poetry of
Mayakovsky, which was not shared by the culturally
conservative Lenin. He displayed his literary values in
his direct interventions in favour of Zamyatin when he
wanted to emigrate, and of Bulgakov when he was out of
work, and he even defended the latter against attacks by
champions of Proletkult.

There is some indication that Stalin was aware of the
literary level of Akhmatova's poetry. It was not by chance
that in the panic-stricken days of autumn 1941 her name
appeared on the list of writers who were to be evacuated
from Leningrad and Moscow when these cities were under
threat. In view of transport limitations, the writers given
priority were those who, according to the 'personal guidelines' laid down by the Central Committee, 'possessed
literary value'. These guidelines were formulated by the
philosopher Georgy Aleksandrov and the list was drawn
up by the literary historian Aleksandr Yegolin; both Party
functionaries were later to play a leading role in the
demolition of Akhmatova's career. The novelist Aleksandr
Fadeyev was responsible for carrying out the evacuations
and reported directly to Stalin on their progress.

There was a story current at this time that when Anna
Akhmatova was ill in hospital with typhus in Tashkent,
Stalin enquired about her state of health ('How is our
nun?'). The result of this concern from the highest quarters was the appearance of a reading lamp above her bed.
Even if this is simply a pleasant fable, it would nevertheless appear to have reflected the essential situation: the

good tsar and the 'mendicant nun' reliant on his favour. In any case it is known that with the help of influential friends Akhmatova obtained a single room in the best hospital in the city at that time – an almost unbelievable privilege indicating intervention at the highest level.

It is possible that Stalin was guided by something like the following considerations. As a statesman who thought on the grand scale, and well versed in literature, he had allowed the forgotten Akhmatova to be resurrected as a poet in 1940. Despite the withdrawal of her book shortly after publication, she had been allowed to remain a member of the Writers' Union. She had spent the war years in the peaceful Uzbek capital. On her return to European Russia in May 1944 she had enjoyed unparalleled fame, responding, admittedly, with a few patriotic poems, but never with a bold, unequivocal Soviet commitment (Bulgakov and Pasternak, by contrast, had not failed to produce direct if purely dutiful acknowledgements to Stalin).

And now this poet had met a representative of an at least potentially hostile major power and meddled in international politics. This must have irritated if not enraged Stalin, and he very probably decided to punish the ingratitude at the first opportunity. Considering that in the Soviet Union public censure was far from being the most severe of possible punishments, Stalin might even have viewed the measures he now took as fair and humane.

When the dictator rhetorically commented to the chairman of the Leningrad Union of Writers that Akhmatova's good poems 'could be counted on the fingers of one hand', he displayed that specifically Soviet attitude to works of art and literature which was characteristic not only of the showdown with the journals *Zvezda* and *Leningrad* but of

Soviet cultural politics in general. Thus after the August Resolution, the closure of *Leningrad* was announced on the specious grounds that there was insufficient talent at this time to guarantee that the pages of two literary journals in Leningrad would be regularly filled. Some years later a drastic economy measure – reduction of the annual number of feature films on general release in the Soviet Union from approximately a hundred to twelve – was introduced with what was seen as the plausible argument that this would substantially lessen the number of 'bad' films.

Although the arguments were mostly specious, the quantitative approach was genuine. A textbook example of Soviet cultural criticism is provided in a speech by Zhdanov in which he takes Vano Muradeli, composer of the opera *The Great Friendship*, to task:

> In this opera not only the wonderfully rich resources of the Moscow Bolshoy Theatre orchestra but also the splendid potential of its singers go unused. That is a great mistake: the talents of the Bolshoy singers should not be buried by confining them to half or two-thirds of an octave when they can command two octaves. Art should not be impoverished.

The laws of economics, of the production of material goods, are here applied to musical composition. Zhdanov makes this connection overtly in his speech at the Smolny Institute:

> Some people find it strange that the Central Committee has taken such strict measures in the matter of literature. Many of us are not used to that. Many people think that if there's a shortfall in production, or the production programme for mass consumer goods or the timber pro-

duction plan is not achieved, then of course a reprimand is in order [assenting laughter in the hall], but if there's a shortfall in the education of youth, then we should just put up with it.

Plainly, the Party functionaries were concerned to guide the literary industry by methods used in economic planning and thus to see that any ideological shortfall was minimized. The Department of Agitation and Propaganda announced one of its triumphs as follows:

In the year 1943 alone, 432 books and pamphlets were removed from the programme of the major publishing houses – as not relevant to the current situation or as inadequately prepared for publication. Many bad books were weeded out when manuscripts and proofs were examined . . . And many newspaper and journal articles were stopped.

Despite such preventive measures, however, literature remained unpredictable. Neither ubiquitous censorship in collaboration with the panic-stricken watchfulness of editors nor the caution of frightened writers could be proof against surprises. When the war was over, a new phenomenon arose: the Soviet people's justified glow of victory threatened to develop into a new civil consciousness. Anyone who had participated in or witnessed the hoisting of the red flag over the German Reichstag was no longer willing, as previously, to obey without question idiotic instructions issuing from uneducated bureaucrats. Many Soviet citizens began to entertain the false notion that certain rights had been won. From this point of view the struggle against Nazi Germany was seen as a service to the state deserving some repayment by the latter.

This was not of course a nation-wide movement, but

simply a swing of public mood. Liberal utterances, however, frequently caused headaches for Party functionaries. The literary historian Aleksandr Yegolin, one of the organizers of Akhmatova's excommunication, reported indignantly to Central Committee Secretary Malenkov in August 1945 that the playwright Vsevolod Vishnevsky, hitherto the personification of Party loyalty, had called out at a plenum of the Writers' Union: 'We fought, we struggled – give us freedom of speech!'

Threats delivered by the local party bureaucracy could achieve little against the danger that lurked in such demands. It was much more effective to make public examples of individuals, take intimidating measures, strengthen old taboos and establish new ones. The most suitable means available to this end was the centrally directed smear campaign.

It was the second summer after the war, the quiet season of cucumber salads. Inland travel restrictions had gradually been relaxed, and there were long queues in front of ticket offices at railway stations.

Anna Akhmatova had remained in Leningrad, where she was alone at this time. She had much to do. Two books of verse were shortly to be published: a substantial selection with the Leningrad state publishing house, with a print run of 10,000 copies, and a slim volume in a series published by the magazine *Ogonyok*, of which the fabulous number of 100,000 copies were to be printed. At the moment when Akhmatova began to check her poems through for these editions, however, the licence for their publication had already been withdrawn. Twelve years were to elapse before publication of her next book.

On the day when the Central Committee Resolution was circulated, Anna Akhmatova went to the offices of the Literature Fund – the institution that dealt with social welfare for writers – to settle some business there. One of those present that day, Silva Gitovich, who later became a close friend of Akhmatova, recalls the admiration of the Fund's employees for her self-control. They were especially impressed by her calm and dignified manner. This was the very day on which she was the subject of virulent abuse in every major newspaper across the whole country. Some years later Akhmatova explained her behaviour on that occasion to Silva Gitovich: 'Good God! I knew nothing whatsoever about it. I hadn't read the morning papers or listened to the radio, and obviously no one had dared to phone me. So I was talking to them [at the Literature Fund] in total ignorance of what had descended on my grey head.'

On the way home, on the Nevsky Prospekt, Anna Akhmatova ran into Mikhail Zoshchenko. From his downcast expression she imagined he had had another row with his wife. 'Just put up with it and carry on,' she urged her companion in fate, without suspecting the relevance of this Christian piece of advice to herself. Then she bought something for lunch and continued on her way back to Fountain House. Only when she reached home and took the pickled herring out of its wrapping did she see her name in the newspaper.

On 15 August Irina Punina went on a trip to Latvia, with her small daughter Anya and her cousin Marina, to visit a relative. She queued for two days to buy rail tickets. When they got to Riga, her six-year-old daughter suddenly said: 'They kept saying "Akhmatova" and "Zoshchenko" on the radio today.' In order to buy tickets back to Leningrad on the black market, Punina had to sell almost all her clothes. It was not until the end of August that she reached home again with her daughter. 'Akuma lay in bed in the large room, saw nobody and spoke to nobody.'

The actress Nina Ardova, with whom Akhmatova usually stayed when in Moscow, was equally taken by surprise. 'I was on holiday with the children in Koktebel,' she explained later in an interview.

> I sent Viktor [her husband] letters and telegrams. I asked how Anna Andreyevna was, whether she had come to Moscow or whether she was going to come. And then I got a telegram from him: 'IDIOT READ PAPERS!' So I read the Resolution . . . I prepared to return home at once. It was difficult to get tickets immediately, with the children . . . I got to Moscow and arranged the journey on to Leningrad. It was several days before I got back to her. I stayed with Anna Andreyevna for three days and then took her back with me to stay with us in Moscow.

Irina Punina recalls that the first thing Akhmatova and Ardova did, almost as a reflex action, was to burn documents, including not only letters and manuscripts but also, very probably, Akhmatova's famous notepads, on which she wrote everything that she didn't wish to speak out loud. A few years later her son Lev was interrogated and maltreated in the Lubyanka specifically with regard to the pile of ashes in which part of his mother's record of her conversations with her closest friend had been found. This burning of papers indicates that Akhmatova expected a house search, and even an arrest was not to be ruled out.

Indeed, many of Akhmatova's contemporaries were surprised that after the Central Committee Resolution of 14 August, Zhdanov's speech of 16 August, and the expulsion from the Writers' Union and the Literature Fund on 4 September, no arrest followed. This relatively mild treatment needs to be considered in the light of the time. Little more than a year after the conclusion of the war the Soviet

Union was still at the zenith of its international standing. Many influential intellectual circles in the West regarded the country, not entirely without reason, as the real victor over Nazi Germany, and therefore – quite unjustifiably – as a basically humane state.

Participation in the Nuremberg Trials, suspension – if short-lived – of the death penalty, comparative tolerance towards the Orthodox Church and, last but not least, the existence of the Jewish Anti-Fascist Committee, all lent the Soviet Union an unprecedented respectability, and foreign policy makers in the Kremlin were now anxious to cultivate this favourable image. At the same time, however, countless thousands of ex-prisoners of war, displaced persons and Cossacks handed back to Russia by the Western Allies continued to be sent indiscriminately to the Siberian camps. But it would have been a grave blow to Western Communist sympathizers and supporters to punish writers at this moment – above all for what they had written.

In the case of Zoshchenko and Akhmatova the Party pursued a restricted and clearly defined aim, that of deterring writers from any kind of heresy, demonstrating that they and their privileges would remain untouched as long as they stuck to the norms of official policy on literature. As a memento of this, a living Zoshchenko and a living Akhmatova were required; the gallows was replaced by the pillory.

Instead of being arrested, Akhmatova was 'shown the instruments'. The Writers' Union stopped her food ration cards for September. This was intended to indicate that Akhmatova's relatively privileged situation as a writer was at an end, and that she was now expunged from social existence. Writers normally received an allowance of up to 500 roubles per month, and a further 200 roubles for taxi fares. Akhmatova now had to rely on the help of her former husband Nikolay Punin, who however, as an art historian, was entitled to no more than a 'scholar's allowance', consisting of food cards to a value of a mere 300 roubles. Furthermore, after 4 September Akhmatova, as a 'former writer', was no longer entitled to a room of her own. Luckily Lev Gumilyov, as a soldier who had fought on the front, could claim a room. The immediate pressure was relieved at the end of September, when Akhmatova received a telephone call from the Writers' Union to tell her she could collect her food cards. In October, with Fadeyev's support, membership of the Literature Fund was restored to her.

The MGB observed Akhmatova's reactions to these measures very closely. One report concluded that she was morally unbroken:

> The subject Akhmatova took the Resolution hard. She was ill for a long time with nervous exhaustion, cardiac arrhythmia and furunculosis. Outwardly she remains cheerful. She has described how people completely unknown to her have sent her flowers and fruit, that no one has turned away from her and no one has betrayed her. 'My fame has only increased,' she has said. 'A martyr's fame. Universal pity and sympathy. Now I am read by people who didn't know my name before. It seems that people turn their backs on prosperity rather than on misery.'

Above all, Akhmatova would not let herself be cowed by the official smear campaign. According to one police source she said of Zoshchenko, hearing that he was suicidal:

> Poor people, they have no idea, or they have forgotten, that it's all happened before, beginning in 1924 [actually

1925, when Akhmatova first heard – from the writer Marietta Shaginyan – of the publication ban on her work]. For Zoshchenko it really was a blow, but for me it just meant more abuse and moral lectures to have to listen to.

Indeed, the powerful Zhdanov had some competition as far as condemnation and denigration of Akhmatova were concerned. In 1925 the critic Viktor Perzov had called her 'a woman who has been born too late or cannot die at the right time'. In Lilya Brik's literary salon, which was tolerated by the authorities, she was spoken of as an 'internal émigrée' at a time when the word 'émigré' carried overtones of treason. It seems to me very probable that Akhmatova made light of the effects of August 1946 on her state of mind in order to deprive her secret antagonists of any satisfaction. Nadezhda Mandelstam's impressions seem to me as if they might be nearer the mark than her own statements:

> Akhmatova's memory preserved the anathema that went back decades, and she received the Resolution in the most appropriate way, that is, without any sign of emotion but with a natural fear of the consequences. She was afraid for her family and for herself as well – impossible not to tremble when a stifling, deadly force draws closer all round you, drags you out of your bed and plunges you into non-existence.

*

Anna Akhmatova once declared that the number of condemnatory pamphlets published about her following the events of the late summer of 1946 was certainly to be reckoned in four figures. The full extent of the filth now poured over the head of this ageing, sick and suffering woman on account of her publications in two regional literary journals may indeed be measured in simple numerical terms. The *Great Soviet Encyclopedia* boasts that in 1946 twenty-six major newspapers were published in the Soviet Union with an overall total of 6.89 million copies sold, with 123 regional daily newspapers selling 3.8 million copies. The total actual readership of the text of Zhdanov's speech when it first appeared in the press must therefore be estimated to have been on the scale of a fair multiple of ten million.

In addition, the text of the Central Committee's Resolution was also printed by all the major journals, some of which had seven-figure print runs, such as *Ogonyok* magazine, the women's paper *Rabotnitsa* (*The Worker* [female]) and the youth magazine *Smena* (*Change*). Zhdanov's speech was also published as a pamphlet with a print run of at least one million copies. More than a hundred major broadcasting stations transmitted both documents; 25 to 30 million Soviet citizens a day heard them on their radios or on the famous public address system. Even after the campaign had died down, the anniversary of the Resolution continued to be observed, and was obligatory study in all secondary schools and the humanities departments of universities and colleges. The infamous words 'nun' and 'whore' were forged into the consciousness of the population in a state of the art ideological campaign.

In the face of this gigantic exercise, the poet had no opportunity for self-defence. She had to listen helplessly when it was claimed that she had remained silent for twenty years after the October Revolution – although in fact silence had been imposed on her. She was condemned for masking her 'inner emptiness' behind an ingeniously coded system in *Poem Without a Hero*, yet she was never allowed to publish the full text of this work in her lifetime.

It was not only writers and literary functionaries who were drawn into this universal hate campaign, but also so-called 'working people', who knew Akhmatova's poetry only from Zhdanov's quotations, people like Comrade Kushner, an engineer at State Factory No. 451:

> You can say one thing about Akhmatova's poems, that this 'lady', who is off her head, is a relic of the old [i.e. pre-revolutionary] intelligentsia which vanished long ago, has no idea of present-day life, and out of sheer idleness just sighs after the past and hinders others from working. The Resolution of the Party CC and Comr. Zhdanov's speech have unmasked these cheap vermin in our literature in good time.

There were also the more subtle arts of falsehood specially designed for liberal Westerners. The Hungarian journalist Iván Boldizsár made a trip to Moscow in spring 1947, and in his book written after the visit he described, evidently in sympathy with his hosts, a press conference at the Writers' Club:

> [Edward] Crankshaw, correspondent for the *News Chronicle*, asks Boris Gorbatov [writer and cultural functionary]: 'So in your country you can only write from a feeling of patriotic duty? About the war, production, heroism?' Gorbatov replies with an obliging smile: 'We can write about anything! The countryside, human beings – or dogs if you like. My friend Prishvin, for example, only writes about dogs, but he likes human beings too. We have the feeling that Mme Akhmatova – she and Zoshchenko had to leave the Union – dislikes human beings, the Soviet people who are now rebuilding their homeland after winning the war.'

Even the highly confidential Party reports on the national mood contain scarcely anything that runs counter to the prevailing atmosphere of an artificially stimulated witch-hunt. But there were refreshing exceptions. One such is provided by the masterly story-writer Konstantin Paustovsky, commissioned by *Pravda* to write a piece on the Resolution. His refusal was as witty as it was brave: 'I'm studying the history of the Party at the moment, and that will keep me busy for some time.' A student of natural sciences at Moscow University named Bashenova, a Komsomol member, is reported as saying to her companions in a group of students who had been stirred by Comrade Zhdanov's speech: 'It didn't do anything for me. I've always loved Akhmatova's poems and I'll go on loving them. You change your minds too quickly – not so long ago you were in raptures over them too.'

Anna Akhmatova, so the anonymous source 'D.D.' states, bore herself stoically: 'It is well known that the women found the Siege of Leningrad easier to endure than the men. Akhmatova was in Tashkent for the first siege, and here [in Leningrad] for the second, the personal one.'

Fortunately for Akhmatova, the personal siege had gaps in it. Outside her immediate household – the Punin family and her son Lev – she had friends of both sexes and admirers around her. Emma Gerstein was at hand, Nina Ardova placed her Moscow house at her disposal at all times, and old admirers like Lev Gornung, who took hundreds of photographs of her, and the poets Olga Berggolts and Margarita Aliger would not allow themselves to be influenced by the stigmatization. And she had one especially close friend – Pushkin; directly after the August Resolution she began to write about *The Stone Guest*. In the 1920s and 1930s Pushkin had already helped her to overcome her severe depressions.

In summer 1948, at Boris Pasternak's instigation, she received 3,000 roubles sick benefit from the Literature Fund. This came just at the right moment; in November she contracted severe inflammation of the lungs. On her recovery she began to translate the letters of the Enlightenment reformer Aleksandr Radishchev, written in French, into Russian – her first literary commission for many years. The book was initially published without her name as translator, but earned a small increase in her meagre income, which was only 700 roubles a month. Her sixtieth birthday was celebrated on 23 June 1949 with her family and closest friends. She was exhausted, ill and depressed, but at last the stranglehold in which she had been forced to live now seemed to have been relaxed a little.

Then on 26 August 1949 Nikolay Punin was arrested. And on 6 November Lev Gumilyov was picked up when returning home from the Museum of Ethnology for his midday meal. The house search was rapidly carried out. Irina Punina recalls:

> Akuma lay in a faint. I helped Lyova pack and got out his sheepskin jacket. He said good-bye to his mother, came into the kitchen to say good-bye to me, and was taken away. The one in charge said to me before he left the flat: 'Please look after Anna Andreyevna, take care of her!' I was quite astounded at this concern. Then they closed the door.

*

Isaiah Berlin learned very little of any of this. When he left Russia his short diplomatic career came to an end and he returned to academic life. Only occasional news from Moscow and Leningrad reached him, and no foreigner dared visit Fountain House.

During our conversation in London Berlin told me he had reproached himself bitterly for Akhmatova's fate and had consciously avoided contacts with the Soviet Union for a number of years. This feeling of guilt is indirectly attested by correspondence from others. One acquaintance, presumably a diplomat, wrote to Berlin as follows, in a letter despatched a few weeks after the August Resolution:

You will have been in a state of anguish at the news of Akhmatova's disgrace – & will I fear have blamed yourself for having in some obscure way contributed to it. In that you will I am sure have been mistaken. A tightening up was to be expected and I don't believe that personal considerations play a part, except perhaps very occasionally as a favourable factor. For even the people in the Kremlin have their human weaknesses sometimes, I think.

Brenda Tripp of the British Council in Moscow wrote to Isaiah Berlin on 12 February 1947 to reassure him that Akhmatova was 'well and living happily and quietly in her flat on a state pension of 600 R. a month'. She too told Berlin that he should not feel responsible for anything that had happened to Akhmatova.

An unidentified correspondent (signed 'Anna') established contact with Boris Pasternak and wrote to Berlin on 19 February 1947. Information about Akhmatova was fragmentary and inexact: 'Anna A. has been allowed to remain in her flat, but has been deprived of her card and therefore material conditions are very hard.' The actual situation was that her food ration cards had been restored, but the authorities were threatening to evict her from her flat. 'Otherwise, as far as B.L. [Boris Leonidovich Pasternak] knows she is all right. The "Bukinisty" have been allowed to sell her books.' This probably refers to her earlier books.

But who are the 'Bukinisty'? The source of this information could only be a 'Bukinist', very likely Gennady Moyzeyevich Rakhlin, 'the tiny red-haired Jew' from whose Writers' Bookshop Isaiah Berlin's path to Fountain House had started.

Anna Akhmatova had written *Poem Without a Hero* in a complex code of allusions, dedications and half-quotations, as a protective cover for its content which detailed the terrible times she had lived through. For the preservation of her central experience and the mythology she built upon it she had only one option – silence. Of this experience she spoke rarely, even to her most intimate friends.

'The secret "Guest from the Future", it seems, prefers to be unnamed,' she declared in 1961 in 'Prose about the Poem'. Anyone who put all Akhmatova's writings on disk and searched for the name of Isaiah Berlin would read 'Not found' on his screen. He was never named.

Yet since the fateful meeting, scarcely a day could have passed on which Anna Akhmatova would not have thought of Isaiah Berlin. The Oxford Professor and Russian Jew from Riga had become, through the very catastrophe of which he had been the unwitting cause, the defining element in the poet's life. Anna Akhmatova, with her extraordinary sensitivity to symbols and cosmic relationships, elevated her meetings with him to a spiritual-ideal plane.

In October 1946 the poet Margarita Aliger visited Akhmatova at Fountain House and found her in a state of the deepest lethargy. She scarcely ever left the flat and had no desire for any contact with the outside world. But then something happened that the visitor had not bargained for.

Anna Andreyevna suddenly said she would like to go out with me. Although it hadn't rained that day, the Leningrad streets were full of their usual autumn dampness and it was squelchy underfoot. We turned off the Fontanka on to the Nevsky Prospekt and found ourselves in front of the Writers' Bookshop. Something caused me to stop in front of the window. Anna Andreyevna suggested we went in and I agreed with pleasure. As soon as we were inside, the cloakroom attendant stopped us and asked us to take off our overshoes. This in fact applied to Anna Andreyevna only; I had rubber shoes on, but she was wearing heavy boots. She said they were difficult to take off, and so it would be better not to go into the shop after all. I should have asked to see someone to have an exception made, but I lost my head. Anyway, even if I had acted otherwise, Anna Akhmatova probably wouldn't have been agreeable. So we continued to walk in the stream of people along the Nevsky.

In this apparently banal event, something scandalous had occurred: one of Russia's greatest writers had been prevented from entering the Writers' Bookshop in her home city. Akhmatova herself could not have been especially affected by the incident; there was nothing to be done in the face of the lust for power of concierges and cloakroom attendants. The occasion, however, marked an important achievement for her: for the first time since her public condemnation she had left the house of her own accord. She took the same route to the Writers' Bookshop that Isaiah Berlin had taken in November 1945, but in the opposite direction. The walk must have reminded her of the meeting, which she thought of, because of its 'disastrous consequences' for her, as filled with a higher significance. And because she 'turned left off the bridge' on her way home, she was obliged, on that day, to look the Guest from the Future in the face. It was surely no coincidence that at this critical moment in her life she devoted all her creative powers to an essay on a subject she had once discussed with Berlin: Pushkin's *Stone Guest*.

Akhmatova divided her poems into those whose origins she knew and those she didn't. There was actually a further category – those she would rather not have written: six in all, belonging to the cycle *In Praise of Peace*, first published in *Ogonyok* in 1949/50. One of these poems bore the title '21 December 1949', Stalin's birthday.

This regrettable cycle was of course forced on her by her son Lev's arrest, and Akhmatova thought of it as a 'petition to the highest name', as petitions addressed to the tsar were once called. She was in the same situation as in the 1930s when, after Lev Gumilyov's first arrest, she began the fifth poem of *Requiem*:

> For seventeen months I've been crying out,
> Calling you home.
> I flung myself at the hangman's feet,
> You are my son and my horror.

For the remainder of her life Anna Akhmatova was tormented by the thought that, if only for one brief, inevitable moment, she had sacrificed her poetic integrity. Her express wish was that the cycle *In Praise of Peace* would never be included in any uncensored edition of her poems, a wish that has not been honoured. As a matter of courtesy I shall make no quotation from this cycle. For, as Yury Tynyanov put it, this is not poetry but 'a literary fact'.

Neither shall I quote directly from another document that testifies to Akhmatova's deep despair in the late autumn of 1949. After Punin's arrest she tried to prevent

Illustration for Requiem *by S. Avakyan*

worse happening by writing a letter to Ilya Ehrenburg in
which she declared her wish to distance herself from her
Western supporters. Ehrenburg sent her letter, together
with some of the poems printed in *Ogonyok*, to Aleksandr
Fadeyev, chairman of the Writers' Union, who in turn
informed Mikhail Suslov, a member of the Politburo, of
Akhmatova's wish. He gave no support, however, to
Akhmatova's request, since the wave of Western anger
provoked by Zhdanov's Resolution now lay more than

two years in the past, and so a public climbdown by Akhmatova 'could be of no great use to us'. Of the poems enclosed he commented in a benevolent but condescending tone: 'They are indifferent poems, abstract, but at the same time they do show some change in her "state of mind".' With these contemptuous quotation marks the matter was closed for Fadeyev. In January 1951 Anna Akhmatova's membership of the Union of Soviet Writers was renewed. A few months later she suffered her first heart attack in Moscow.

In 1949 Lev Gumilyov was sentenced to ten years' labour camp in Siberia, first in Karaganda and later near Omsk, actually being released in 1956. Neither his mother's poems nor her petitions had been of any help to him.

The last great Stalinist wave of terror was almost arbitrary. The bookseller Rakhlin was among those arrested in the 1948 campaign against 'rootless cosmopolitans', meaning Jewish intellectuals. He was accused of clandestine contact with Golda Meir, Israel's first ambassador to the Soviet Union, during a visit she paid to Leningrad. Even local Party leaders who had played a part in the excommunication of Akhmatova and Zoshchenko were victims of this purge. Many of them lost their lives in the so-called 'Leningrad Affair'.

In 1994 the historian Gennady Kostyrchenko, in the course of research on the 'anti-Zionist campaign', unearthed extensive details of another terrible affair. In the summer of 1950 the KGB arrested a number of doctors on the staff of the Moscow Dietological Clinic, including the director, Dr Pevsner, who was a relative of Mendel Berlin, father of Isaiah. Dr Pevsner and Mendel Berlin had met at the beginning of the 1930s in Karlsbad, which the Moscow doctor was visiting on professional business. In the inflamed imaginations of KGB functionaries, the private meeting of these two men was part of a far-reaching conspiracy. Pevsner was said to have volunteered for the British secret service of which Mendel Berlin was alleged to be a representative. 'Confessions' obtained from Dr Pevsner by torture 'incriminated' Mendel's brother Lev, a doctor at the same Moscow clinic.

According to Isaiah Berlin, his father, the businessman Mendel Berlin, re-entered his native country for the first time since the October Revolution in 1935. Details of his stay in Moscow, and of his visits to his brother, were carefully noted by the NKVD. Ten years later the then foreign minister Molotov made an attempt to refuse Isaiah Berlin's diplomatic accreditation with the comment: 'We don't want any of the old ones', by which he meant former citizens of tsarist Russia. This attempt was successfully diverted by Molotov's advisers, who pointed out that the foreign diplomat in question had been a child during the October Revolution. However, Berlin, who wished to go to Moscow in June, had to wait until 8 September for official recognition as a staff member of the British Embassy. We can be sure that the KGB watched the new First Secretary from first to last with special vigilance. It is inconceivable that a meeting between nephew and uncle would have gone unobserved.

Dr Lev Berlin was arrested in January 1952 and sentenced to twenty-five years in a labour camp for 'spying'. Later, during the currency of the 'theory' that secret services of the imperialist powers had set up the Jewish doctors to give Soviet leaders, including Stalin, 'fatal treatment', Dr Berlin was brought back from Siberia to Moscow and tortured for four days to make him 'confess' to having been a middleman between the Jewish 'conspirators' and the 'British spy' Isaiah Berlin. Lev Berlin had the perfect alibi, however, regarding Stalin's death – he was not released from labour camp until the spring of 1954.

These events, about which Isaiah Berlin must have learned during his second visit to Russia at the latest, could only have strengthened his assumption that any approaches he made in the Soviet Union could have catastrophic consequences – not a reassuring thought for a citizen of a democratic state. The Soviet Union, in its criminal role of hostage-taker, had succeeded in extending the frontiers of tyranny to Oxford.

3 'Oxford' Students in Leningrad

On 6 March 1953 the literati of Leningrad assembled at the House of Writers, also known as the Mayakovsky Club, to commemorate Stalin, who had just died. Anna Akhmatova was present; she was a member of the Union of Writers, and her absence would have been an immense affront. She did not join in the ostentatious mourning of her numerous colleagues, though she could not have been unaware of the historic consequences of this moment.

The period immediately following Stalin's death was characterized, after the title of a short story by Ilya Ehrenburg, as The Thaw. A few years later the film director Grigory Chukhray made use of this metaphor in the film *Blue Skies*. Huge breaking ice-floes and rivers bursting into flood stamped the consciousness of a whole generation.

And indeed, the beginning of de-Stalinization had the character of some mighty natural phenomenon. Stalin's death created a power vacuum. In the struggle that followed, his would-be successors made haste to fill the breach. Events took on a strange double aspect. The protagonists acted for the most part not according to chosen criteria but rather to the logic of power. But they were often caught up in the dynamic of the process itself. For example, at the end of March 1953 Lavrenty Beria released the Jewish doctors who had been arrested a few weeks earlier, accused of murdering a number of Soviet leaders including Zhdanov. He aimed by this ploy to weaken his KGB opponents, but it turned out to hasten his own fall and subsequent execution.

'Recently I have often woken up in the night for joy,' Anna Akhmatova told her friend Lydia Chukovskaya in April 1953. This feeling was a response to the release of the Jewish doctors, the last hapless victims of a Stalin smear campaign. Something overwhelming had indeed occurred: *Pravda* had condemned the torture method by which the doctors' confessions had been extracted.

The mere fact that the organ of the Party had lived up to its name and, astonishingly, printed the truth, would have been sufficient grounds for jubilation. Anna Akhmatova, however, hoped for further miracles – the release of her son Lev and her former husband Nikolay Punin. The charges against both, after all, were just as fictitious as those against the Kremlin doctors. Akhmatova might also have reckoned that the highly propitious Thaw would undermine the Party Resolution of 1946 and even sweep it away.

She was not alone in these hopes. In autumn 1953 Korney Chukovsky wrote in his diary: 'I've been to see Fedin. He says a new spring has arrived in literature . . . A whole book by Akhmatova is to be published, a whole book, with old and new poems.'

Staying with the Ardovs in Bolshaya Ordinka Street, as she usually did when in Moscow, Akhmatova had one day been called for by a chauffeur-driven car and taken to the offices of the largest of the state literary publishers, Khudozhestvennaya Literatura, where she had been treated with great deference and given a clear undertaking that a selection of her poems would be published, the first since the slim volume published in Tashkent in 1943.

The moving spirit behind this initiative was Aleksey Surkov, First Secretary of the Union of Soviet Writers since 1953. At times in the past when Akhmatova had been the victim of persecution, slander and discrimination, Surkov had seen his task as damage-limitation. Now he wished to have justice done to her.

In order to understand a figure like Surkov, good and evil must be regarded not as opposites but as parts of one inseparable whole. Surkov was a special Soviet case of Molière's *bourgeois gentilhomme*. He worked heart and soul for a system that had a pathological fear of every unfettered word, and so especially of poetry. At the same time he had a good ear, if not perfect pitch, for genuine poetry. Over the years he developed into a double agent: the spy for poetry in the corridors of power, and simultaneously an uncompromising representative of Party interests in literature. He played this double role, especially in regard to Anna Akhmatova, with undeniable charm. He brought her flowers whenever he went to see her, so that she always called him 'the bridegroom' when speaking of him. But this bridegroom's marriage-settlement was similar to Nicholas I's in his rapprochement with Pushkin: 'I will be your censor.'

As a young student in Moscow in 1963–4 I often found myself in the presence of Aleksey Surkov at the well-attended evening readings at the House of Writers in Vorovsky Street. He took the chair with the freshness of a newly peeled egg, face aglow with rude health, hair snow-white, surrounded by well-known Soviet and foreign writers – the Russian Margarita Aliger, the Bulgarian Yelizaveta Bagryana, the young German Hans Magnus Enzensberger, the Pakistani poet Faiz Ahmad Faiz, and my fellow countryman Ferenc Juhász. Surkov was in his element when presiding over these occasions, relishing the role of *tamada*, Caucasian host. He must have been glad to spend a few brief hours not having to disseminate official lies as the country's highest cultural diplomat, supporting Joseph Brodsky's expulsion from the country or justifying Lev Gumilyov's latest arrest.

*

In the years following Stalin's death Western interest in the Soviet Union grew, and Kremlin foreign policy responded accordingly. A policy of modest *détente* at the time of cease-fires in Korea and Vietnam and the first summit confer-ences in Geneva was also pursued at the cultural level. The first guest performances of the Bolshoy Ballet and concerts by the country's most famous musicians were intended to promote the image of *détente* and convey the impression that, politically and economically, 'everything was normal' inside the Soviet Union.

Foreign interest in writers like Akhmatova, Pasternak and Zoshchenko could earn propaganda points for the Soviet system. At the same time there was a danger that the class enemy would pick out only what fitted the arsenal of the Cold War, and would not be prepared to accept the overall picture of Soviet literature which Soviet leaders wished to convey. The Soviet propaganda machine was staffed almost exclusively by ideologues of the classic Stalinist era and was completely unprepared for the sub-tleties of this new situation. Out of all this was to come the next demoralizing blow to Akhmatova's career.

Not long after Stalin's death a delegation of Soviet writers led by Surkov visited the Leipzig College of Literature. The students, visibly stimulated by the 'new direction' that had been imposed on the East German Communist Party, the SED, put some ticklish questions to the delegation from the land of Big Brother. More than twenty years later the East German poet Adolf Endler was inspired by this occa-sion to write a poem which he dedicated to the song-writer Bettina Wegner, whose songs had been banned at the time.

Visit from Moscow, 1954
or: Asking about Akhmatova

Fadeyev! – Paustovsky! – Korneychuk!
Isakovsky! – Bashan! – Shchipachov! –
Ketlinskaya! Kasil! Katayev!

'Ah – is Akhmatova still alive?'

Bek! – Lebedev-Kumach! – Syomushkin!
Sholokhov! – Polevoy! – Lugovskoy!
Surkov! – Shaginyan! – Libedinsky!

'And is Akhmatova still alive?'

Pervomaysky! – Fedin! – Lukonin!
She's still alive, just listen!
Aseyev! – Ashayev! – Fadeyev!

'So she's still alive, Akhmatova?'

*

'Is Akhmatova still alive?' – This question was also asked
by members of a student delegation drawn from several
British universities which accepted an invitation from the
Anti-Fascist Committee of Soviet Youth and the All-Union
Association for Cultural Contacts Abroad (VOKS). Its two-
week tour of the 'Homeland of the Workers of the World'
in the spring of 1954 was one of those half-tourist, half-
propaganda events by which the Soviets sought to make
themselves popular with foreign intellectuals.

Professor Harry Shukman of Oxford described the trip to
me in 1995; he had been an undergraduate at Nottingham
University at the time. 'We stayed at the Metropol in
Moscow. Every meal was a banquet. People were wary of
speaking to us. They lived in great poverty.'

The party consisted of about twenty students, Shukman being the only Russian-speaker. First they besieged their interpreter with questions, then they proceeded to set about their official hosts. In the Lenin Library there was almost a row. 'It's Orwell and Trotsky we're interested in,' we told them, 'not the works of Lenin. Where is Dostoyevsky? We were incessantly provocative, so much so that I think their attitude towards people like us must have been very different after this meeting. We really laid into them, we really did.'

After other tense exchanges of this sort the party arrived in Leningrad at the beginning of May. There the revolutionary young tourists insisted on a meeting with the two disgraced writers Akhmatova and Zoshchenko. The Soviet side agreed to a meeting on 5 May at the Mayakovsky Club.

In summer 1953, at the funeral of the painter A.A. Osmyorkin in Moscow, Anna Akhmatova met the famous architect Lev Rudnev, designer of the Moscow University building completed in the same year. Rudnev was a friend of Marshal Voroshilov, who, appointed Chairman of the Presidium of the Supreme Soviet after Stalin's death, was official head of state. Rudnev promised to ensure that Akhmatova's plea for clemency for her son Lev would reach Voroshilov, which it did by February 1954.

Anna Akhmatova regularly went to Moscow at this time to seek her son's release. She had to get train tickets from the Writers' Union, and phoned for this purpose on 4 May 1954, whereupon she was asked to come to the Leningrad House of Writers the following day for a meeting with a party of English students. A functionary named Katerli phoned an hour later with the same request. Akhmatova searched for pretexts to get out of the invitation, but met with an uncompromising response:

'You absolutely have to come, or they will say you have been strangled.'

Four days later, Akhmatova described the event to her friend Chukovskaya in Moscow:

They sent a car to take me there. The Red Hall we know so well. A crowd of English students, very few Russians. Sitting there were Sayanov, Zoshchenko, Dymshits . . . and me. And the interpreter, a girl from VOKS – all very formal. I sat looking at them all, examining their faces – who was who? I knew a catastrophe was brewing for me, but I didn't know who would put the questions. First they asked about book publishing: What was the institution that authorized publication? Did it take long for books to come out? What did the censors demand? Could you publish a book yourself [*sami izdat'*], if it was rejected by the publishing houses? Sayanov gave the answers. Then they asked if policy towards literature was *now* any different from 1946. Whether there'd been any going back on the speech [Zhdanov's] and the Resolution. Dymshits spoke. It was interesting for me to hear the answer 'No', there had been no change at all. Then the brave pirates went over to the attack and asked Mr Zoshchenko to say what his feelings were about the Central Committee Resolution of 1946. Mikhail Mikhaylovich answered that at first he had been shocked by the injustice of the Resolution, and had even written a letter to Josef Vissarionovich to say so, but that later he had understood that a good deal in the document was right . . . There was light applause. I waited. Someone in dark glasses was asking the questions. Perhaps he didn't wear glasses at all and it only seemed to me that he did. He asked what Mme Akhmatova's feelings about the Resolution had been. He invited me to reply for myself. I stood up and said: 'Both Comrade

Zhdanov's speech and the Resolution of the Central Committee of the Party are in my opinion absolutely correct.'

Silence . . . Then one of the Russians turned to the interpreter: 'Would you please ask them why they applauded Zoshchenko and not Mme Akhmatova?' 'We didn't like her answer,' they said, or they might have said: 'We didn't like her.'

The then Party Secretary of the Leningrad Region, someone called Kazmin, gave a similar description of this meeting in the report he was asked to send to the Cultural Department of the Central Committee in Moscow.

The discussion lasted three and a half hours. One of the English students declared that he was no supporter of the Soviet system. For the rest, there were numerous questions of a provocative nature. For example: Why were portraits of leaders displayed everywhere in the Soviet Union, and posters appealing for higher productivity and sporting records? Didn't it all bore people to death? Why were the works of such great writers as Dostoyevsky not published? What were the relations between writers and the Government? How did literary works come to be written – were they commissioned or did writers write what they wanted? Why did Soviet students have so little knowledge of English literature? . . . All these questions were answered precisely and correctly, and the latest Soviet edition of the works of Dostoyevsky was displayed.

Then this question was put to Akhmatova and Zoshchenko: 'You were criticized in Zhdanov's speech. What do you think, without going against your conscience – was that criticism right or not?' Zoshchenko answered that he hadn't agreed with the criticism and had therefore written to J.V. Stalin. Then in a confused speech he tried to give the reasons why he had not agreed with the criticism . . . His answer was received with applause by the English delegation.

Next Akhmatova spoke. She stated laconically that the Central Committee Resolution and Zhdanov's criticism had been correct: 'That was my understanding at the time. And that's still my understanding today.' There was no applause after this.

'I knew a catastrophe was brewing for me,' said Anna Akhmatova of this occasion. In fact, two catastrophes were to occur – her own and a greater one for Mikhail Zoshchenko. What happened to Akhmatova that afternoon was essentially a repetition of previous experience. In 1940 and 1949 too she had hoped that a symbolic demonstration of loyalty to the system would win release from prison camp or at least a mitigation of sentence for her son. Each time she deceived herself, for Lev Gumilyov was treated by the system as a straightforward hostage rather than an object of barter. Akhmatova's informal overtures were just as unsuccessful in achieving her aim this time as on previous occasions; President Voroshilov preferred not to intervene personally for her son, but instead diverted her plea to the 'appropriate quarters'.

In contrast to her earlier concessions towards the system, this time Akhmatova's attempt at a display of loyalty relegated her to outer darkness. The lack of applause for her words signified that she had disappointed a foreign audience. She herself was convinced of the inevitability of her answer, but in view of the attitude of her colleague and fellow victim Zoshchenko, palpable pressure for some self-justification weighed on her.

Emma Gerstein recalls Akhmatova's desolate feeling of insecurity at the time. In fundamental literary terms, as she observes quite rightly though almost apologetically, the lyric poet and the humorist had scarcely anything in common, and it was only the Central Committee Resolution of August 1946 that happened to bring them together.

> Eight years later the two of them were invited to a discussion with students from Oxford who had come to the Soviet Union as tourists . . . Subsequently, Anna Andreyevna, of course, was very indignant at the crass contrast that had been made between her response and Zoshchenko's. 'He has no son in a camp,' she repeated many times. When she spoke of her appearance that day she would stress the casualness, show how she had sat 'half-turned away' from the audience and told them in extremely few words that she 'completely agreed both with the Resolution and Comrade Zhdanov's speech'. In this way, so it seemed to her, she had indicated to the students that she did not wish to discuss her political situation with them.

In the summer of 1955, when Zoshchenko, once more being harassed, even if this time only semi-publicly, by Party committees, was a psychological wreck, Akhmatova said to Lydia Chukovskaya:

> Mikhail Mikhaylovich is much more naïve than I thought. He actually imagined that it was possible to explain something to them in this situation . . . In cases like this, you can only give the sort of answer that I did. Can and must. In no other way. We were unlucky. If I'd answered first and he second, my answer would have shown him that he should have answered in the same way. No subtleties, no psychology. Then he would have avoided disaster. But he was asked first.

I don't think that Anna Akhmatova would have been able to influence Zoshchenko's answer to the students' question. As he said later, in a passionate speech of self-justification, his open riposte to the organizers of the event was a purely emotional act:

> What could I have answered? What was I to say? Anna Andreyevna said: 'I agree.' The charges against her were different. In her place I'd probably have given the same answer as she did! But what am I to answer if I'm asked if I am an un-Soviet writer, who makes fun of Soviet man – if I am asked if I'm a baddy? . . . What does this question mean – 'What do you think of being called a hypocrite?' . . .
>
> Perhaps this question was a provocative one? Perhaps they wanted to make me agree with it and say: 'Yes, I am a cheat, I am an un-Soviet writer . . . I don't care about my life any more! I won't ask you any favours! I don't need your favours, I don't need your shouts and abuse! I'm more than exhausted! I'll accept any fate that comes to me!'

There are borderline situations in which alternative moral actions are possible. Zoshchenko's appearances at the Mayakovsky Club and subsequently at the Writers' Union were unquestionably heroic. For the first time since the 1920s, a writer openly confronted the degrading cultural bureaucracy and went on the offensive in demanding his human rights. In this sense Zoshchenko proved to be a direct forerunner of all the writers who rejected the humiliating rituals of self-criticism in the ensuing decades and later questioned the moral legitimacy of the system itself.

Acknowledgement of Zoshchenko's heroism does not detract in the slightest from Akhmatova's courage. This is especially to be stressed in view of the legends that sprang up decades later with *perestroika*. The novelist and story-writer Andrey Bitov, for example, is supposed to have said of his colleague, after the meeting with the English students: 'Look where she's left me!' Even if Bitov really said this, it was entirely unjustified. It would have been impossible for Zoshchenko and Akhmatova to have agreed on any common line. The words probably spring from the conscience of one of those eternal voyeurs of the catastrophes of others. At the same time, on neither Zoshchenko's nor Akhmatova's part was there ever any sign that either would have given up their mutual solidarity.

Nadezhda Mandelstam, in the second volume of her memoirs, *Hope Abandoned* – her source is probably Akhmatova – writing of the meeting that had such fateful consequences for Zoshchenko, comments on the students:

It is said that they were sent by Berlin, the Oxford 'Guest from the Future', who had visited Akhmatova shortly before the whole drama that overtook her . . . Had these Oxford students understood Akhmatova's behaviour? . . . These nice English boys, brought up always to tell the truth and stick to their opinions, must have been confused when they heard Akhmatova say that the Resolution had been of great benefit to her. Comparing this statement with the poems from *Ogonyok*, they must have taken the Russians for a wholly corrupt people, who can be bought for a kopek. Or perhaps they caught a glimpse of the secret, Asiatic Russian soul, with its love of Resolutions, poverty, prison camps and executions . . . They understand us about as well as we understand the Chinese.

Lydia Chukovskaya writes more caustically of the inquisitive guests from Albion:

> What sort of English people are these – utter ignor-
> amuses, dimwits, scoundrels, or are they blind? Why did
> they have to poke their fingers into other people's pain?
> Here were people who had been thrashed and humili-
> ated, and what did they ask: 'Do you like being
> thrashed? Show us your broken bones!'

Only the British biographer and close friend of
Akhmatova, Amanda Haight, takes a more charitable view
of the students' behaviour at the Mayakovsky Club, seeing
it as 'the misplaced well-wishing of a group of foreigners
who had no real idea of the situation as seen "from
inside"'.

These summary judgements, however, are surely unjustified. The young Britons were neither 'reactionary and
anti-Soviet', as their hosts later stated, nor did they wish
to 'poke their fingers into other people's pain', as Lydia
Chukovskaya accuses them of doing. They behaved in
accordance with the norms of the free world, the only ones
they knew, and their student temperament was not very
different from that of John Osborne's 'Angry Young Man'
who was to confront the British Establishment two years
later in *Look Back in Anger*. Perhaps for the first time in their
lives, they had the opportunity to distinguish between
oppression and freedom with their own eyes – and what
normal young person was to resist such a temptation? Of
course, their desire to uncover the whole truth at a stroke
was naïve and tragicomic. However, that was hardly their
fault, but rather that of a perverse and unknown world of
whose rules they had no inkling.

How were the meeting and Akhmatova's behaviour per-
ceived by the students themselves? In August 1995 Harry
Shukman gave me the following account, differing significantly from Akhmatova's in the matter of her reply to the
leading question:

The situation in the House of Writers was completely artificial. There was no exchange of views between us and the writers. Akhmatova said nothing. And then I asked: 'Perhaps Mme Akhmatova would like to say something?' But she didn't want to. It was clear from her expression that she didn't want to say anything, she was nervous. I asked again: 'What do you think of what Zoshchenko said?' She said: 'I agree.' That struck us as ambiguous – she might have been referring to Zoshchenko or to the Resolution. I still remember the scene as if it were yesterday. She wouldn't be pinned down as to whether she meant Zoshchenko or the Resolution . . . The atmosphere at this meeting was pretty, how shall I say, tense.

Eleven years later, when Anna Akhmatova visited Oxford to receive an honorary doctorate, Harry Shukman, erstwhile undergraduate of Nottingham University, was among the hundreds of the poet's admirers present. 'She stayed at this hotel,' he recalled in the foyer of the Randolph, where we had arranged to meet.

I was invited to the reception for her. The University was the official host, but Isaiah Berlin played the main role . . . He had invited all the Slavists in Oxford to attend the evening. A great number of people, including me. She sat alone on a divan, and Berlin had stipulated that anyone who wanted to speak to her had, say, five minutes. Then the next person. There was an informal queue. I stood there, and I must tell you, I felt very uneasy with myself. But I knew that if I didn't say anything to her, I shouldn't have a clear conscience afterwards.

I told her I had been present at the meeting with the students in Leningrad and asked her if she still remembered it. 'How could I not remember it?' she answered.

'Zoshchenko didn't survive that occasion.' 'My God,' I said. She looked at me and I said: 'I asked the question.' She replied: 'And why did you ask it?' I said: 'Out of naïvety, a desire to be able to compare not so much a dissident as an independently minded writer with those who toed the Party line.' She said: 'I understand.' That was all.

Here I should like to draw attention to a point that may have escaped the reader's attention. Akhmatova's closest friends and her first biographer Amanda Haight, in speaking of this affair, refer to 'students from Oxford', 'a delegation from Oxford', and Nadezhda Mandelstam was even of the opinion that they had somehow been sent, with appropriate instructions, by Isaiah Berlin. This was a view shared by many contemporaries. Chukovskaya alone among Akhmatova's friends and acquaintances consistently refers to the group as 'English' students.*

I am told by Harry Shukman that all major universities were represented in the twenty-strong delegation from the National Union of Students – except Oxford and Cambridge. Shukman had no preparatory contact with Isaiah Berlin; the two did not meet until 1958.

In the course of our discussion in London, Berlin denied that there had been any contact whatsoever between himself and the members of the student delegation of 1954; he had heard about their visit only after the event. Following the Central Committee's Resolution of August 1946, Berlin avoided any further meeting with Akhmatova for fear of adding to her troubles.

* Roberta Reeder, in her introduction to *The Complete Poems of Anna Akhmatova* (1990) and her biography *Anna Akhmatova: Poet and Prophet* (1994), puts the record straight, referring in the former to 'A group of twenty British students – none from Oxford, and definitely not sent by Isaiah Berlin'. – *Translator.*

All this may be the objective truth, but it plays no part in the subjective background to the meeting with the delegation. The false label 'Oxford Students', as Lydia Chukovskaya told me in 1995, could only have come from Akhmatova herself. If her assumption that the students had come from Oxford was patently an error, it was, if I may be allowed the romantic expression, an error of the heart.

For Anna Akhmatova, as for every Russian brought up before the Revolution, the name of Oxford had a very special ring. It stood for the culture of the British intellectual aristocracy, and to be a professor at this university was to have attained the highest possible intellectual prestige. Akhmatova was evidently well aware of the status of an Oxford honorary degree. Her literary secretary, Pavel Luknitsky, who was also, as it later turned out, the police informer personally assigned to her, reported that once, while involved in the strenuous labour of helping her second husband Shileyko copy out inscriptions on Assyrian clay tablets, she remarked: 'When you're wearing ermine at Oxford University, remember me in your prayers!'

After November 1945 Akhmatova elevated the habitual Oxford myth to a new formula: Oxford = Isaiah Berlin. When the cultural bureaucrat Katerli spoke to her of 'English students', Akhmatova automatically associated them with Oxford, and welcomed the opportunity of taking a look at these young people who breathed the same air of freedom as Isaiah Berlin and for that reason alone were ambassadors of the Guest from the Future – although at the beginning of the telephone conversation with Katerli she made the mock-pathetic suggestion that some other old woman might be introduced to the students. In fact, she had no choice in the matter.

Those three hours, therefore, that Anna Akhmatova

spent sitting between the Party puppets Dymshits and Sayanov must have been double torture. Once again she had to force herself to cast aside the proud role of resistance fighter, that in which Isaiah Berlin had come to know her. And once again she was placed in the distressing and obscene position of having to choose between Berlin, the man whom she idolized, and her son. In her eyes the former was the incarnation of life as it should be, the latter personified what life actually was.

The official view was that the meeting in the Leningrad Writers' Club was a definite slip-up on the Party's part. The Potemkin Village* required for such a meeting was erected too hastily, and collapsed equally prematurely. The organizers had omitted to attend to what had hitherto been an essential part of the repertoire of state – ideological preparation of victims for their role. In his report of 27 May 1954 Comrade Kazmin washed his hands of the affair; he knew very well that mishaps of this sort had already cost Leningrad functionaries dear.

It must be pointed out that the Party organization under the Chairman of the Leningrad Branch of the Soviet Union of Writers has brought to light gross irresponsibility in the handling of the organization of the meeting between the writers Zoshchenko and Akhmatova and the delegation of anti-Soviet English students. This meeting was not agreed with the Regional Party Committee. Although the views of the English student delegation were known beforehand to employees of the Regional Komsomol Committee, the latter nevertheless

*This phrase, originally denoting fake villages put up by Potemkin, Catherine the Great's viceroy, in newly annexed territory in the south of Russia in order to make it look more populated than it actually was, has entered other languages besides Russian. – *Translator*.

acted irresponsibly in going ahead with organizing the meeting. It is recommended that stricter control be exercised in future in regard to all events connected with the reception of foreign visitors.

Party leaders scented a coming scandal. On their return home the students could be expected to give publicity to the unsuccessful Soviet cultural propaganda attempt. The Party was therefore careful in taking its next step. Zoshchenko was summoned before the plenary committee of the Writers' Union in an effort to make him recant. But the immediate cause of the present fuss was kept from the public. The average reader of *Leningradskaya Pravda* on 28 May 1954 therefore did not understand a word of D.W. Druzin's fulminations:

> Those present at the Party meeting are of the opinion that even in Leningrad there are some writers who clearly have an incorrect attitude . . . Zoshchenko, for example, has learnt no lessons from the Central Committee's Resolution *On the Journals 'Zvezda' and 'Leningrad'*. Recent events have shown that Mr Zoshchenko has concealed what he really thinks about this Resolution and still holds his corrupt views.

Passions roused by the fiasco only died down on 7 August, when an article about the visit by one of the students in the delegation appeared in the *New Statesman and Nation*, under the title 'A Student in the USSR'. The author, the Chilean student Claudio Véliz – described by Harry Shukman as 'the only Marxist in our delegation' – wrote of his visit to the Lenin Library in the following terms:

> A visit to the famous Lenin Library of Moscow, reputed to contain over seventeen million volumes, reveals the

degree of intellectual censorship to which the average Soviet reader is subjected; the catalogue of works in English does not contain a single book by James Joyce or Virginia Woolf, and, of course, nothing by Koestler, Orwell or Isaac Deutscher. Eventually, one of the librarians took me to a catalogue on the fourteenth floor. Here I found not only the works of Joyce and Forster, but also *Animal Farm*, *Homage to Catalonia*, Deutscher's *Stalin*, and every book that one can possibly think might be frowned upon by the Soviet authorities. This catalogue, the librarian told me, was open only to 'specialists'.

For all his criticism of Soviet practice, Véliz was in general satisfied with what he found in the Soviet Union. He had been especially impressed by what appeared to him to be a lack of taboos on subjects of public discussion. One student had sharply criticized Beria, who had already been executed; another had even dared to call Zhdanov's Resolution – he too was dead by this time – 'stupid'. Véliz said not a word about Zoshchenko or Akhmatova, or the fact that millions filled the prison camps of the country he had visited. He wrote in the same pseudo-objective tone as the left-wing Lion Feuchtwanger in his account of a visit to Russia (complete with a meeting with Stalin), *Moscow 1937*.

The Moscow newspaper *Izvestiya* was equally satisfied with Véliz for his performance. An article by its London correspondent W. Matveyeva appeared on 7 September 1954, commenting:

Talking to people in the Soviet Union showed these English students that the claim that free, unforced discussion is impossible in the Soviet Union is pure invention. On the contrary – Véliz had lively and in-depth discussions with everyone he met in the Soviet Union, on all the subjects that interested him.

Sheer relief over the disaster that didn't happen put the lords of culture in sunny mood. Zoshchenko, now mentally destroyed, was given a month in a sanatorium at the Black Sea spa of Sochi, and in autumn 1956 a volume of his stories was published. It was all too late, however. He had two years to live.

Thanks to his journalistic brilliance Mikhail Zoshchenko had been used to a much wider public than Anna Akhmatova. In the 1920s and 1930s he often worked for dozens of newspapers and journals simultaneously, each for separate fees. His sayings were on everyone's lips the next day. When membership of the Writers' Union was restored to him in the autumn of 1953, his hopes were similar to Akhmatova's. Publication of a cycle of novellas in the Moscow journal *Oktyabr* had been agreed.

After the meeting with the English students at the Mayakovsky Club, Zoshchenko's world collapsed. Directly after the June meeting of the Writers' Union, he got a polite telegram from the editorial department at *Oktyabr* saying: 'We very much regret to tell you that your stories are not suitable for our journal.' When he complained to the Leningrad branch of the Writers' Union he was told – or such was his impression – that his work was never to be published again, 'regardless of its quality'. At the same time it was suggested to him that it would be appropriate to write a 'clarifying letter' to the Central Committee, a new humiliation. He was in a predicament uncannily similar to that of August 1946. But 'poor Mishenka', as Akhmatova put it, 'didn't get through the second round.'

Lydia Chukovskaya, paying him a visit in Leningrad in the late summer of 1955 to give him money from her father, found him in a pitiful state.

Mikhail Mikhaylovich is so thin that he is unrecognizable, all his clothes hang off him. The most extraordin-

ary thing is that he seems completely ageless, he is a
shadow of himself, and shadows have no age . . . His
voice is toneless . . . 'The most degrading thing for me is
that no one gives me any work,' he says. 'I don't care
about anything else.'

What had happened was desperate and grotesque. A
completely pointless local propaganda campaign had been
waged; it went wrong, but without damage to the Party.
Three months later, all the song and dance, all the
'scandal', was over, one couldn't say that anything in particular had happened. Two people's lives, however, had
been almost destroyed, one of them never to recover. And
a year later, one final lie was all that remained of the whole
affair.

In March 1955 the young writer and Party propagandist
Sergey Saligin paid a visit to a prison camp in Omsk to
lecture to the inmates on the latest developments in Soviet
literature. The period after Stalin's death saw a marked
increase in the provision of political and cultural events
in the gulag. One of the inmates, Lev Gumilyov, later
described Saligin's lecture to Emma Gerstein: 'I asked him
about Mama. He said she was experiencing a "creative
upsurge", and that English students had visited her to
enquire about her health.' Since Gumilyov thought that
his mother was insufficiently concerned about him, this
reply injected a little more poison into the bad blood that
already existed between him and his mother.

If Saligin's statement had been intended for liberal
Western periodicals like the *New Statesman and Nation*, it
would have been a bare-faced, cynical lie emanating from
the Soviet opinion-formers. The mollifying remark was
addressed, however, to a camp prisoner, a citizen of the
third class at best, and consequently had special significance. It was made in the year 1955. No one knew

whether someone who was starving in the gulag today might not be released tomorrow and take up some high-ranking position. The mass liberation of political prisoners was just beginning. Every day brought the moment nearer when, in Akhmatova's words, two Russias would confont each other – the one that was serving sentence and the one that was delivering it. In this sense Saligin's deliberate lie was a first modest sign of that weakening of the system that surfaced in the spring of 1956 as criticism of Stalin and eventually, in the late 1980s, as collapse.

4 *The Non-Meeting*

The treasury of classic Soviet anecdotes contains one remark attributed to the writer Lev Kassil. In 1952, after the death from natural causes of a highly placed Party boss, this successful author of books for the young is supposed to have said: 'So even people like him get heart attacks.' This statement may sound banal to Western ears, but at the time it hit the mark, shaking the myth of the higher *nomenklatura*. Artificially cut off from the rest of the population, surrounded by an aura of secret power, these iron men were nevertheless vulnerable to illness – provided they escaped the next purge. The acknowledgement that they were ordinary mortals must have sounded almost revolutionary in the period before Stalin's death.

The placing of the Georgian's body beside Lenin's in the crypt of the Mausoleum in Red Square saw the end of the latest despotism in Russian history. The power struggle that immediately ensued set the hitherto stalled political carousel in motion again. Every day someone in the hierarchy was dismissed from office or transferred to another post, sometimes serving as a public scapegoat. The humiliating loss of inviolability was suffered by office-holders at all levels.

In March 1955 the careers of the most senior cultural bureaucrat of the Central Committee, Aleksandr Yegolin, and the Soviet Minister of Culture, Georgy Aleksandrov, suddenly ended when they were found guilty of running a private brothel for themselves and other senior officials at a dacha outside Moscow, with students of the Maxim Gorky Literary Institute as prostitutes.

These two disgraced officials had each had an influence on Akhmatova's career. Aleksandrov had been involved in the banning of the volume *From Six Books*, and Yegolin had assiduously provided information and quotations used in the preparation of the Resolution against the journals *Zvezda* and *Leningrad*, for which he had been rewarded with the editorship of *Zvezda*, which continued publication after a purge of its staff.

The rumours about the orgies laid on by Yegolin and Aleksandrov passed round writers' circles like wildfire. Korney Chukovsky was incensed above all by the softness of the Party reprimand of Zhdanov's ghostwriter, the scholarly literary historian Yegolin, restricted as it was to his sexual excesses. 'How can such a parasite be condemned just for that,' he wrote in his diary, 'and not because he "edited" the works of Chekhov, Nekrasov [the nineteenth-century poet] and Ushinsky [the nineteenth-century educational theorist] without lifting a finger himself but getting others to do the work, and was paid more for this "editorial work" than Chekhov, Nekrasov and Ushinsky earned in their entire lives.' When news of the once mighty bureaucrat reached him some years later, he could not contain his anger: 'He was at Zhdanov's side during the outrageous campaign against Akhmatova and Zoshchenko and went about Leningrad like an executioner's assistant.'

The list of Yegolin's sins, especially regarding his financial greed, may be extended. He had dressed up his research work for Zhdanov, for example, into an article, published it in *Zvezda* under his own editorship of the journal, using the pseudonym Yelyugin, and received a fee for it. In the proceedings against him this kind of brazenness was totally ignored, as were the demands of some writers and CP members that he should be expelled from the Party for his sexual immorality.

Anna Akhmatova responded to her antagonist's fall from grace with a single sentence, seeming to express a limp gesture of the hand: 'And *Yegolin* found my poems indecent.' Perhaps she already sensed what kind of justice, despite the rehabilitations getting under way, was to be expected from the new old masters of the Kremlin.

The liberation of political prisoners from the gulag was a process that lasted several years, owing to the huge number of prisoners and the limited capacity of the Soviet legal system. The mass arrests and executions of the late 1930s had been carried out with the help of a drastically simplified and accelerated procedure. A hearing at a special session of the Military Tribunal, which might end with a sentence of death or twenty-five years in a labour camp without the right to correspond, often lasted no longer than twenty minutes. Cases claiming restoration of rights, on the other hand, could not proceed with comparable swiftness.

Above all, clear judicial criteria were lacking. Who was to be given rehabilitation and who the more limited grant of amnesty? What was to be done about secondary sentences for released prisoners, for example the ban on entry to principal cities? The fundamental problem, however, lay deeper. How could hundreds of thousands of victims of injustice be declared innocent without opening the question of collective responsibility throughout the system? Those who had once made the decisions as well as those who had carried them out were still alive and in office. It was hardly surprising that they did everything possible to ensure that the Thaw, when it came, should melt only the tip of the iceberg.

Outright political, judicial and moral rehabilitation was

reserved almost exclusively for former members of the
Party apparatus or the officer corps, and even while Stalin
was being denounced, these 'tens of thousands' of unjustly
persecuted Communists were the only released prisoners
in this category. A second category of rehabilitation was
that granted to artists and scientists according to their
degree of fame and proximity to the official cultural élite.
The best that all others below this level could hope for
during the years of de-Stalinization – millions of workers
and peasants, priests, soldiers, Cossacks, homosexuals,
draft-dodgers, abortionists and their clients, even whole
ethnic groups like Chechens and Kalmucks – was release
with their bare lives.

Intellectuals like the art historian Nikolay Punin and
the ethnologist Lev Gumilyov belonged to the category of
'class enemies', and were not automatically accorded
state pardon. To obtain their release, *khlopoty* – special
efforts – were necessary, intensive intercession with the
authorities. All important victims of Stalinism were of
course released after the CPSU 20th Party Congress of
1956 at the latest, but for them and their dependants
the timing of release during the period 1953–6 could be
significant.

Nikolay Punin did not live to experience his rehabilitation. He died on 21 August 1953 in a camp at Vorkuta in
the north 'of natural causes', a phrase merely denoting
that he was not directly murdered. Although their relationship was long since over, Punin's death was a severe
shock for Anna Akhmatova. She had always accepted
Punin as part of her life, shared a flat with his former and
present family, and in turn been part of his life. The
release of her son Lev, furthermore, had now become
more than a simple matter of time; he was ill, and each
successive day he spent in camp could result in his sharing
Punin's fate.

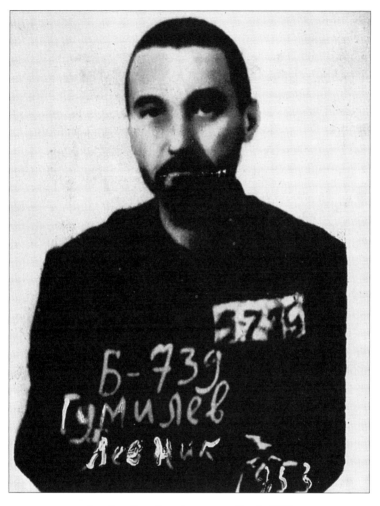

Lev Gumilyov in prison camp, Omsk, 1953

In spite of the intervention of certain prominent academics on Lev's behalf, his release was an intolerably long time in coming. As there were many such unresolved cases and the danger of prison uprisings steadily increased, a special commission was set up, chaired by Anastas

Mikoyan, a member of the Politburo, to speed up the liberation of camp inmates. It brought about Gumilyov's release, although it was some months before he received formal rehabilitation.

Impatiently, almost despairingly, Akhmatova awaited the decision on her son's release. Not until the end of March 1956 was she able to breathe a sigh of relief, and ask her closest friends shrewdly: 'Is it true that you can get a good man's suit for 800 roubles?' On 15 May, in the Moscow flat of the Ardov family, mother and son met again after six and a half years' separation. Soon after this joyful reunion, however, conflict broke out between them, which lasted until Akhmatova's death. As so often in the Soviet Union, shortage of living space caused the first friction.

Lev had been arrested in Fountain House, in the flat where he was legally registered but where he did not have a room to himself. When in March 1952 the landlords, the Institute of Polar Research, probably in co-operation with the secret police, forced the Punin–Akhmatova household out of these premises, they were allotted a smaller flat on Krasnaya Konnitsa. In 1955, as a member of the Literature Fund, Akhmatova was given a small dacha in Komarovo near Leningrad, of minute size, which she called 'the cabin'. When Lev returned he did not have the automatic right to be registered in the Punin household, and Akhmatova could offer him only Komarovo. He refused to live there, however, and, now homeless, felt rejected by his mother.

In letters written to Emma Gerstein from the gulag, Lev Gumilyov had already maintained that his mother had shown insufficient concern for him and made inadequate efforts to obtain his release. He voiced the same charges, with undiminished feeling, when speaking about Akhmatova in an interview in 1989.

She never actually made an application seeking my release, therefore it was impossible to make any real attempt to get me out. When I came home from the camp in Omsk I asked her why she hadn't made an application. She couldn't give me any real answer, although she took a women's course in law in Kiev in 1910.* Mama never learned that every case had to begin with an application, or, as it was called in those days, a petition . . . My mother never fully understood this.

This absurdly naïve line of argument is easy to refute. That a pre-revolutionary law course, or any part of one, would have been a preparation for attempting to confront the Soviet system of injustice in 1949 or even 1954 was a complete fantasy, born of a mind that had been frustrated and unhappy for decades on end. It was not so much that Lev missed Akhmatova's petitions during his years in the gulag, but rather that throughout his life he had felt deprived of the normal care and concern that average sons of ordinary mothers are entitled to expect. In the break between mother and son that took place in the late 1950s, the emotional deprivations of Lev's childhood, which he spent with his paternal grandparents, came home to roost.

Lev Gumilyov, the gifted son of a woman of genius, grew up in the shadow of a father who had been executed, and spent thirteen of the most productive years of his life behind barbed wire. Any one of these external circumstances would have been quite enough to make him a mental cripple. His real undoing, however, was that – apart from his 'original sin' of 1934, when he had read Mandelstam's satirical poem on Stalin aloud to a group of

*Akhmatova actually entered the Kiev College for Women to study law in 1907, but did not finish the course. – *Translator.*

friends – he was not responsible for his own fate. It was forced on him by his origins.

From his earliest youth, Lev Gumilyov's parentage lay upon him like an enormous weight. 'My mother always told me: If I wanted to be her son, then above all I had to be my father's son,' he said at one interrogation. He was unable to live up to these high demands. He broke down under interrogation and subscribed to every statement required of him, as did the great majority of the victims of Stalinism, except for a few isolated heroes. In the gulag he was subjected to questioning about Isaiah Berlin. We have an account of this from Emma Gerstein, describing his final homecoming:

> I shall probably astonish Sir Isaiah when I say that Leva was very harshly questioned on the foreign diplomat's visit to his mother. For some days after his return home, when everything was still in a turmoil in his mind, Leva couldn't give a coherent account of what he had had to go through during those years. All the more convincing were the words that poured out of him uncontrollably. He was tormented, for example, because he had spoken disparagingly of Anna Andreyevna when he was inter-rogated about the fateful visit: 'Mama was the victim of her own vanity' . . . Once Leva involuntarily recalled how his interrogator had seized him by the hair, banged his head against the hard wall of the Lefortovo prison and forced him to admit that Akhmatova had carried out espionage for England.

It wasn't surprising, therefore, that on return from the gulag Lev Gumilyov, although he had harmed no one except himself, was tormented by self-reproach. His mother too suffered from guilt feelings. While she thought of everything that had happened to her since 1917 as, to a

certain extent, a tragic-heroic 'deserved fate', the fulfil-
ment of which gave her moral satisfaction, as regards
Lev's quite unheroic years in labour camp she suffered
for the rest of her life from an agonizing pressure for self-
justification.

In summer 1956 Isaiah Berlin visited Moscow once more,
spending several weeks, with his new wife Aline, née de
Gunzbourg, as the private guest of the British and
American ambassadors. He looked up old friends. But
before he decided to renew contact with Anna
Akhmatova, he consulted his closest Russian friend, Boris
Pasternak.

The first thing he was told was that *Doctor Zhivago*, in
process of composition at the time of Berlin's first visit to
Moscow, was now completed. Pasternak had had the
manuscript smuggled to Italy, where it was to be published
by Feltrinelli in Milan. In view of the fact that the novel
had been simultaneously condemned by more than a
dozen Soviet editors in an 'internal review' as 'counter-
revolutionary, shoddy work', the consequences of publication in the West were not difficult to foresee.

The scandal of the 'Pasternak Affair', when the poet was
awarded the Nobel Prize for Literature but was forced by
the Soviet authorities to decline it, was still two years off.
During the summer of 1956 Pasternak was in a state of
high excitement. This is important to mention, because
his mood unquestionably influenced his British visitor's
behaviour.

Isaiah Berlin recalled his conversation about Akhmatova
with Pasternak at this time:

Pasternak told me that though Anna Andreyevna
wished to see me, her son, who had been rearrested
some time after I had met him, had been released from

his prison camp only a short while before, and she therefore felt nervous of seeing foreigners, particularly as she
attributed the furious onslaught upon her by the Party
at least in part to my visit in 1945. Pasternak said that he
doubted whether my visit had done her any harm, but
since she evidently believed that it had, and had been
advised to avoid compromising associations, she could
not see me . . .

Up to this point, what Pasternak had said to Berlin had
been rational enough. Then, however, according to Berlin's
account, Pasternak continued: 'but she [Akhmatova]
wished me to telephone her – this was safe, since all her
telephone calls were certainly monitored, as were his
own.'
The word 'since' in this statement takes us into the
world of fairytale, East European phobic fantasy. It indicated that the speakers could gain the upper hand over the
listener-in by freely exchanging emotionally sincere statements in the latter's hearing, against which the evil
authorities would be powerless. Even Pasternak seemed
confused by this theory of Akhmatova's, adding obscurely
and illogically that Berlin should phone Akhmatova not
from the British Embassy or from his, Pasternak's flat but
'from a public phone booth'.
   All this has to be taken into account if the psychological
background to the dramatic event referred to in
Akhmatova's poetry and Akhmatova literature as the
'Non-Meeting' is to be at all understood. She and Berlin
were staying in Moscow at the same time, and could quite
well have met by chance in the street or at the house of a
mutual acquaintance.
   Most sources agree that Akhmatova ruled out a meeting
with Berlin because she feared that another meeting with
him might harm her recently released son. Although such

a fear would seem unjustified in the circumstances of the time, it was by no means wholly without foundation. It was the burnt child's fear of fire, undiminished over a life-time.

When in 1956 her brother Mikhail Gorenko sent her a letter from the United States for the first time for many decades, Akhmatova was so frightened that she went to the 'Big House', the KGB office in Leningrad, to enquire whether she was entitled to receive mail from abroad. The KGB told her that she was. Towards the very end of her life, in May 1962, universally acknowledged in her own country at last, she still complied when a minor bureaucrat from the Leningrad Writers' Union advised her to refuse an audience to certain American journalists under the pretext of illness. Even in summer 1965, at the high-point of her triumphal visit to Oxford, she was tormented by fears that after her return home, as after her visit to Italy the previous year, she would be politely questioned by a KGB officer about her impressions.

The fear of meeting foreigners was natural, given the officially imposed xenophobia in Soviet society. In this sense Akhmatova's refusal to see Berlin was simply a reflex conformity to internalized norms. Nadezhda Mandelstam explains the decision in philosophical terms: 'The cause of the "Non-Meeting" was tangible and real: the artificial barrier put up between the two worlds, the impenetrable wall, the impassable ditch ... People who had something to say to each other were absolutely separated in space.'

In 1995 the literary historian Emma Gerstein, in her nineties and living in Moscow, expressed the view that a meeting between Akhmatova and Berlin would have been perfectly possible in 1956, and that it was prevented entirely by Pasternak's irrational fears, which Berlin took over wholesale. 'The friendly service that Boris

Leonidovich performed for Anna Andreyevna,' says Gerstein ironically,

> placed him [Berlin] in an awkward situation – like a gentleman to whom a lady has refused an audience. All the more so because he had here become caught up in a political system that, in the eyes of a representative of a European country with a highly developed sense of the rule of law, must have seemed wholly bizarre. Both partners in the dialogue forgot what they had seen of Soviet life with their own eyes, and their clear perception of its irrational basis. Here true feeling for history betrayed them, and they looked for sober rationality where it had never been and never could be.

A second possible reason why Anna Akhmatova refused to see the 'Guest from the Future' again might have been wounded pride – or more precisely, disappointment in love.

Pasternak called Akhmatova before Berlin did and told her tactfully that Berlin was not alone in Moscow, but was accompanied by his new wife, who was charming. It was then that the model telephone conversation took place, no doubt with the security precautions devised by the overcautious author of *Doctor Zhivago*, a book that made all precautions pointless. Berlin recalls the conversation with Akhmatova:

> Later that day I spoke to her over the telephone. 'Yes, Pasternak told me that you were in Moscow with your wife. I cannot see you, for reasons which you will understand only too well. We can speak like this because then they know. How long have you been married?' 'Not long,' I said. 'But exactly when were you married?' 'In February of this year.' 'Is she English, or perhaps

American?' 'No, she is half French, half Russian.' 'I see.' There followed a long silence. 'I am sorry you cannot see me, Pasternak says your wife is charming.' Another long silence.

Berlin correctly pointed out on a number of occasions – our meeting in London was one of them – that his version of this telephone conversation differed from Akhmatova's. There is in truth scarcely any factual contradiction between the two accounts, but there is certainly an emotional gulf between them. What Akhmatova revealed to Lydia Chukovskaya on 23 August 1956 was no less than an addition to her long series of tragedies:

A man called me on the telephone – of course you know who I mean, you and one or two others know all about it – and was quite astonished when I said I couldn't see him. But he should have realized himself that *after everything* I can't expose myself to new risks . . . He told me some interesting news: he got married only last year. Just imagine what kind of respect that shows for me – *last year*! I thought it would be too banal to congratulate him. I said: 'Well, good!', and he replied . . . well, I won't tell you what he replied . . .

The implications of what had occurred were not lost on Chukovskaya: 'Although her words had a mocking tone, she spoke in a deep, slow voice heavy with suffering, and I realized that she had called me that day for the express purpose of telling me about this "non-meeting", that she had just taken another most difficult decision.'

Many Russian writers have believed in the mystique of numbers. The singer-poet Vladimir Vysotsky composed a song linking specific numbers with the fates of poets:

Pushkin was thirty-seven when he was killed in a duel; Mayakovsky shot himself at the same age; Rimbaud and Byron died in their thirty-seventh year. Vysotsky himself was thirty-seven when he wrote this song, and the number thirty-seven further symbolized the Great Terror for him.

Anna Akhmatova's numerology also contained special dates and their symbolic connections. She established that the day on which Khrushchev was forced to resign, 14 October 1964, was the hundred-and-fiftieth anniversary of the date of birth of the poet Lermontov (1814–41), the hundredth anniversary of whose death in 1941 was also the day of the Nazi attack on the Soviet Union. Akhmatova died on 5 March, the same date as Stalin thirteen years earlier. According to the literary critic Lev Ozerov, Akhmatova suffered her fourth and last heart attack while reading an article in *Pravda* on the seventieth anniversary of the birth of Andrey Zhdanov (1896–1948). Without denying the capacity of the central organ of the CPSU to produce heart attacks, it should be noted that Akhmatova's took place on 10 November 1965, when she had to be taken immediately to the Botkin Hospital.

Akhmatova felt strongly that the most painful experiences of her life occurred in August. Her literary master Aleksandr Blok died on 7 August 1921. Eighteen days later her former husband Nikolay Gumilyov was executed. The infamous Central Committee Resolution of 1946 was dated 14 August. Nikolay Punin was arrested in Fountain House on 26 August 1949 and died in the gulag on 21 August 1953. Only her son's arrests (October 1935, March 1938 and November 1949) did not fit this scheme.

The last symbolic number to be considered here will serve as a guide in the search for further reasons to explain the Non-Meeting. On 14 August 1956, the tenth anniversary of her excommunication, in the dacha of her friends

the Shervinsky family near Moscow, Akhmatova wrote a
poem entitled 'A Dream', which she later included in the
cycle *Sweetbrier in Blossom*. Here is the first indication that
something unusual and significant had just occurred:

> O my August, how could you give
> Such news on this terrible Anniversary!

Nine days later Lydia Chukovskaya recorded in her diary
the account Akhmatova gave her of the telephone
conversation with Berlin. The same source reveals that
Chukovskaya and Akhmatova met on 15 or 16 August,
after the latter had come to Moscow. Akhmatova made no
mention at all of Berlin. To her friend's question whether
things had gone well at the Shervinskys, she replied
'reproachfully': 'Can things go well for me anywhere?'
'And then I noticed,' runs Chukovskaya's diary entry,
'how tired her eyes were.'

But what was the 'news' that had reached her on 14
August? The above-quoted lines are from a poem which, as
its title implies, is about a dream. Its opening quatrain ends
with the line: 'And that same night I had a dream of your
arrival.' Why 'dream of'? Berlin had arrived in Moscow in
reality. By painstaking research it would no doubt be possible to establish the exact time of his landing at Vnukovo.
Akhmatova, however, is writing of another event:

> It was in everything . . . in the Bach Chaconne,
> And in the roses, which bloomed in vain . . .
>
> And in the autumn, which came close
> And suddenly, reconsidering, concealed itself.

Undoubtedly, someone had arrived who had already been
with her before. The Bach Chaconne, a motif used earlier

by Akhmatova, is an unequivocal indication of the appearance of the Guest from the Future at Fountain House. Music, whether by Bach or Vivaldi, is one of the mystical planes on which Akhmatova imagined herself as meeting her loved one.

And now out of this dream a real man approached her, whom she did not wish to meet in reality.

It may be that Akhmatova refused to see Berlin again out of concern for the fate of her son, wounded pride, or a mixture of both. As a poet, however, she is expressing another feeling – despair:

> How shall I pay back this royal present?
> Where shall I go and with whom shall I celebrate?

This is the utterance of someone who is destitute and who awaits a wealthy guest. A few days later, on 18 August, she writes as if wanting to clear up a misunderstanding or warn of a bitter disappointment:

> You invented me. There is no such person,
> There could be no such person on earth.
> . . .
> You and I met in an improbable year,
> When the powers of the world had already dried up,
> Everything was in mourning, everything wilted from
>   suffering,
> And only the graves were fresh.
> . . .
> So it was then my voice sent for you.
> What I did I could not understand myself.

Independently of Akhmatova the woman, who might have good grounds for or against a meeting with Berlin the man, Akhmatova the poet shows an uneasiness with the

Guest from the Future. He had first come to meet her, she declares, because she had called for him. Their meeting had been once and for all, historic. What, therefore, would a further meeting achieve?

Akhmatova waited until 14 September, when Berlin had returned to Oxford, before showing these two poems, numbers 6 and 8 in the sequence *Sweetbrier in Blossom*, to Lydia Chukovskaya, saying: 'Both of them were finished when I last saw you, but I didn't trust myself to read them to you. And no one says anything to me about them. Please say two words – you can say things about poetry.' Chukovskaya replied: 'I'll say precisely two words: great poems.' 'No worse than my early poems?' 'Better.'

Akhmatova got exactly the answer she was seeking, fulfilling her almost naïve wish to earn the highest possible praise for these two poems from the person who knew her poetry best. Why then had she so long denied herself the success that she so intensely desired? And why did she at first seek it by showing the poems to other readers, who would only have been able to respond to work written with her heart's blood with a polite and banal 'Beautiful'? More precisely: why did she describe, on 23 August, the Non-Meeting, and only afterwards the two poems about it that had been written '*before*' that Non-Meeting? It seems to me that at the time of writing the two poems, on 14 and 18 August respectively, she already knew that Isaiah Berlin was in Moscow, but couldn't decide what to do. And she did not want Chukovskaya, familiar as she was with every aspect of her life, to know of her inner turmoil.

The concept of the Non-Meeting arose immediately after the telephone conversation with Berlin, and at the outset it acquired an attribute that was typical of Anna Akhmatova – that of secrecy.

> The celebrations of the secret
> Non-meeting are empty.
> Unspoken speech,
> Unpronounced words.
> Uncrossed glances
> Do not know where to land,
> And only tears are happy
> Because they can flow and flow.

It is difficult to avoid the impression that the poet, here giving her happy tears free vent, is really celebrating a triumph. The Non-Meeting was 'secret' because it contained Akhmatova's secret within it. It was part and parcel of the Guest from the Future, just as strategically important production centres and their employees were part and parcel of the State. She declared the Guest from the Future 'top secret', according him this status in August 1956: 'The secret Guest from the Future prefers to remain unnamed.' This was no wish, but an order.

At the same time, Akhmatova was concerned to establish the closest possible relationship with Berlin. 'He won't become my dear husband,' she wrote in the Third and Last Dedication to *Poem Without a Hero*; and in lines that originally belonged to the poem 'In a Dream' (not to be confused with 'A Dream', also in the cycle *Sweetbrier in Blossom*), she wrote more directly:

> Dear friend, we shall never share
> What Our Lord commanded us to share,
> We shall not spread the table-cloth,
> We shall not put a pie on it.

The relationship here conjured up in the negative is unquestionably something very like marriage. I am certain that in November 1945 Akhmatova would not have considered this an impossible idea. Her imagination accepted neither conventions nor national barriers. She lived what she felt in her dreamworlds. Least of all would she have been influenced by the age difference, which she regarded simply as a matter of cosmic chance, as a love-poem written at the age of seventy-five shows:

> It was a mistake for us to see that year in,
> Absolutely wrong.
> My God, what did you and I do?
> With whom did we exchange fates?
>
> It would be better for us not to be alive,
> Better to be in heaven's Kremlin –
> We flew like birds and bloomed like flowers,
> But we were still just you and I.

At such a spiritualized level, love can no longer be threatened by worldly powers; not even Stalin could have succeeded in that. The appearance of Isaiah Berlin in person would very likely have disrupted this transcendence. In August 1956, therefore, Akhmatova banished him to the world of her dreams, and perhaps this had less to do with love than with the right to her own tragedy. A further meeting with Berlin would have relativized the tragedy, lowered the drama of fate to the level of anecdote.

The price for this kind of relationship, however, was high. For years Akhmatova awaited a mystic message:

> At least today give me a call,
> Since you are, at any rate, somewhere,
> But I have become the most homeless of the
>   homeless,
> And I don't get any news at all.
>
>   *
>
> It's a long time since I believed the telephone,
> The radio, or the telegraph.
>
>   *

The assumption that a meeting with 'the foreigner' – as Nadezhda Mandelstam calls Berlin, a note of inner frostiness creeping in – might cause further difficulties for Lev Gumilyov was an unlikely one in the year 1956. The revoking of any amnesties would have meant abandoning the line taken at the 20th Party Congress, and the immediate fall of Khrushchev.

Other problems, however, weighed on Akhmatova. Her translation work earned what was by Soviet standards a high if irregular income. She hated these commissions with all her heart – she worked mostly on literal versions of poems from Chinese, Korean, Romanian and Bulgarian. Without her earnings from this work, however, she would have been condemned to the same miserable level of existence as the great majority of Soviet pensioners.

Journal or volume publication of her poems was beset with still greater pressure and irritation. Some idea of the obstacles and difficulties involved may be gained if the publication date of the slim volume *Poems*, 5 November 1958, is compared with the date of delivery of the manuscript to the publishers, 21 October 1953.

The unusually long period before publication was due in this instance not only to a neurotically over-sensitive censorship that scented intentions hostile to the state in every line, but above all to Akhmatova's unresolved status. In brief, the Akhmatova Problem was part of the Zhdanov Problem. For her position to be restored at least to what it had been before August 1946, the Zhdanov Resolution would first have had to be reviewed.

Had Andrey Zhdanov lived to attend the 20th Party Congress of February 1956, and spoken against Khrushchev's secret speech – which he might well have done, in view of his fanatical faithfulness to the 'Chief' – then, like Molotov and Kaganovich later, he would have been expelled from the Party. In that case the Party, with light heart, would have pinned the blame for all the errors of earlier cultural politics on him, and Anna Akhmatova, provided she remained loyal, would have attained, if not national renown, at least official recognition. The dead Zhdanov, however, occupied a hypothetical place in the de-Stalinization process, a place where, absurdly, things were harder to cope with than Stalin himself.

The Soviet leadership was especially averse to any attempt to see the operation of principle in the murderous events of the Stalin period – to attribute them to anything other than historical chance or the consequences of the dictator's capricious character. When the leader of the Italian Communist Party, Palmiro Togliatti, interviewed by the journal *Nuovi Argumenti* in May 1956, speaking of the Great Terror, referred to 'certain forms of distortion' of Socialism, the Soviet Communist Party responded with an angry Central Committee Resolution. Equally angrily, the Soviet Communist Party rejected the Yugoslav Party's condemnation of Stalin's theory and practice as 'Stalinism'.

Critical Russian intellectuals did not use this term either, preferring the old Russian suffix *-shchina*. *Stalinshchina* had the same ring as *Hitlerei* (Hitlerism) to German ears, though the roots of the suffix were deeper. All earlier *-shchinas* of Russian history, for example the infamous *Arakhcheyevshchina*, denoting the mindless suppression of the spirit of freedom by Nicholas I's minister of police, had a contemptuous ring, which did not accord with the official view of Stalin's 'merits and flaws'.

When on 15 June 1956, at a writers' conference, the Turkish poet Nazim Hikmet, living in exile in Moscow, labelled Soviet cultural politics of the early 1950s *Zhdanovshchina* for the first time, he met with firm resistance from conformist writers. One of the few of those present to support him was Akhmatova's close friend the lyric poet Olga Berggolts. As a Party member she had to watch her words, but she left no doubt as to her essential meaning.

> Among the greatest problems that still weigh on us and hinder our progress, I am certain, are all those dogmatic resolutions of the years 1946–8 about art . . . Comrades, let us be perfectly frank about these.
>
> Why now still? Now of all times, when, after the 20th Party Congress and Comr. Khrushchev's speech on the personality cult, it has become clear to us that those resolutions were the expression of Stalin's personal taste, that is to say, they were simply consequences of the personality cult.

The Party leadership was worried, but was afraid of engaging in open polemics, which would have provoked manifestations of sympathy for the writers it attacked. The literary bureaucrat B. Ryurikov, writing in *Pravda*, therefore left his target, Olga Berggolts, anonymous. 'There are *some* writers,' he wrote in the Party's central organ at the end of August,

> who try to represent the well-known Resolutions of the Central Committee on questions of literature and art as no longer valid. These Party Resolutions, however, are directed against the separation of literature from the life of the people, from the political tasks of our time, against those who forget the transformative social role of art – and we will defend these fundamental principles contained in our Party documents in the interests of the development of Soviet literature.

It was characteristic of this formalized Party language that no form of words or omission was a matter of chance.

When Ryurikov spoke in the first sentence of 'literature and art' but of 'literature' alone in the last, this indicated that the Party had recently come to adopt a slightly less strict stance *vis-à-vis* the non-verbal arts. And indeed, ten years later Zhdanov's resolution of 10 February 1948 on music, which can be regarded as his swan-song, was officially rescinded in favour of another Central Committee resolution.

What was the reason for this generosity of Party spirit? Most Party documents mingled irrational figments of imagination and rational fears. Zhdanov's resolution criticizing Shostakovich, Prokofiev, Khachaturian, Muradeli and other composers was a prime example. I have already quoted, from Zhdanov's attack on Muradeli's opera *The Great Friendship*, the near-classic passage criticizing the composer for under-exploiting the orchestral and vocal resources of the Bolshoy, and ending with the words: 'Art should not be impoverished.'

Alongside this conventional stupidity, Zhdanov addressed the most serious concerns of *raison d'état*.

The opera shows us the struggle for the establishment of friendship between the north Caucasian peoples in 1918–20. The mountain peoples, amongst whom the opera attempts to represent the Ossetes, Lezghi and Georgians, progress ... from struggle against the Russian people ... to peace and friendship with them. The historical distortion here lies in the fact that these peoples *were not hostile* to the Russians [Zhdanov's emphasis]. It was the Chechens and the Ingush at that time who were obstacles to the friendship of peoples in the northern Caucasus.

It is a matter of historical fact that in autumn 1944 the Soviet government got rid of these 'obstacles', the

Chechens and the Ingush, by brute force. Not until 1956 were the sad remnants of these peoples, who had been transported to Siberia, allowed back to their homelands. Place-names like Grozny, Budyonnovsk and Pervomay-skoye are today bloody symbols of how that half-hearted rehabilitation achieved precisely the opposite of 'great friendship' in the Caucasus. But from the Soviet point of view the episode seemed over at the time, and so Zhdanov's tirade, not otherwise overloaded with content, had lost all relevance to present events. As Oscar Wilde didn't say, art, or in this case official art criticism, imitates life.

Which was not the case with Party resolutions on liter-ature. Zhdanov's documents, aside from their primitive crudity, contained unreconstructed Leninist thinking. In the first place, writers, more than other kinds of artist, were thought of as channels of ideological instruction. In the second place, the severity of Zhdanov's resolutions was directed against concepts of the enemy that did not lose their impact or official validity until 1988. The perennial targets, 'bourgeois decadence', 'cosmopolitanism' and 'bowing and scraping to the West', were easiest to strike at in written texts.

The condemnation of mass executions and mass arrests in the Stalin era implied the Party's promise never to allow atrocities on such a scale to occur again, and despite their natural urge towards the use of force, the Kremlin leaders after Stalin kept this promise. At the same time, the 20th Party Congress brought no fundamental relaxation of the practice of political and moral execution of oppon-ents, as was to be seen in the cases of Zoshchenko and Akhmatova. Such a relaxation would have meant renunciation of the tried and tested method of public denigration and professional banning of writers, a concession that the Soviet Communist Party would have found hard to make.

Anyway, legalization of criticism of the euphemistically termed 'personality cult' by itself had the effect of unleashing conflicting energies in the cultural domain, as a secret report of the Cultural Department of the CPSU entitled *On Questions of Contemporary Literature and Incorrect Attitudes among Some Writers* testifies:

> In the Literature Faculty of Moscow University a wall newspaper was recently displayed that was full of extravagant praises for three writers who were said to be the 'greatest' of the present age – Pasternak, Tsvetayeva and Akhmatova. It is significant that none of the Communist academic staff was bold enough to speak against this biased and deviant tendency among the students of the Literature Faculty, refute it critically, and show up its bad taste.

The growing concern of the literary-political authorities is partly explained by the circumstances of the time: the Soviet Army had recently marched into Hungary to put down a popular rising in the preparations for which rebellious writers had taken part. Literary unrest was considered dangerous to the community, and to be handled with appropriate care.

Hence the first critical reappraisal of Zhdanov's Resolution of 14 August 1946, if only for internal use:

> The Resolution on the journals *Zvezda* and *Leningrad* contains assessments and characterizations which were incorrect and in need of greater precision in the context of statements of the personality cult in recent years on the question of the guidance of literature and art. Unnecessary regulations, an administrative tone and

fuss crept in, a certain rudeness to authors and artists who had made mistakes in their work.

As is often the case with Soviet ideological statements, one part of the message is cancelled out by another:

At the same time the content of the Central Committee Resolutions on the journals *Zvezda* and *Leningrad* and the repertoires of dramatic theatres is basically correct, and the most important points made in them still retain their validity today. The struggle to achieve an elevated level of ideas in literature, the struggle against apolitical attitudes, poverty of ideas, pessimism, and bowing and scraping, the requirement to study the life and needs of the Soviet people more deeply, to explain the fundamental questions of our time, to educate our youth through art so that it becomes livelier, more cheerful and truer to its country, believes in the victory of our cause, and fears no difficulties – all this was and remains the most important task that faces writers and artists.

Thus the condemnation of Anna Akhmatova was not basically reversed. In theory she was allowed to publish once more, but every censor, publisher's reader or editor had the right to reject her work on the authority of the Central Committee Resolution on *Zvezda* and *Leningrad*, one of these journals having long since been forced to toe the Party line and the other having ceased publication ten years previously.

After Pasternak's warnings, the telephone conversation between Akhmatova and Berlin on 23 August 1956 was so well-conducted that even the most rigorous listeners in the Lubyanka were unable to find fault with it. Akhmatova spoke with gentle mockery of her retranslations of verse from the Korean, and described her problems during the excommunication of ten years previously, when some of her friends had turned away from her while others had remained faithful. She did her best to preserve a calm, dispassionate tone throughout. A single remark of hers stands out from this conversation, which we have in Berlin's account: 'she had reread Chekhov . . . and said that at least in *Ward No. 6* he had described her situation accurately, hers and that of many others.'

Chekhov had been an important theme of the nocturnal conversations of November 1945. Akhmatova had then made one of her magisterial and sweepingly unjust statements, denouncing Chekhov, Berlin recalled, because 'his universe was uniformly drab; the sun never shone, no swords flashed, everything was covered by a horrible grey mist – Chekhov's world was a sea of mud with wretched human creatures caught in it helplessly – it was a travesty of life.'

If there is any one work by Chekhov regarding which Akhmatova's criticism hits the mark uncannily closely, it is *Ward No. 6*. The action of this story written in 1892 takes place in the psychiatric 'annex' of a hospital in a small provincial Russian town. Here the patients vegetate, hopelessly and for decades on end, to the complete indifference of society and the doctors and terrorized by the sadistic warden Nikita, who thrashes them with and without cause.

Life outside the hospital is scarcely any better. The head doctor, Andrey Yefimich Ragin, a cultivated man and a confirmed bachelor, is tired of his work and suffers from chronic boredom and loneliness. To his misfortune, among the psychiatric patients he makes the acquaintance of the young bailiff Ivan Dmitrich Gromov, placed in the annex on account of his persecution mania. In his lucid moments

Akhmatova at the time of the Non-Meeting, 1956

Ivan Dmitrich proves to be the companion in conversation whom Ragin has long wanted. Doctor and patient do not reach agreement in their philosophical arguments, but Ragin makes the young man what is almost a declaration of love:

'The point is this – we can both think; we see in each other people capable of thought and judgement, and that gives us solidarity together, however different our individual views may be. If only you knew, my friend, how tired I am of apathy and lack of intellect and talent, and how happy I am when we talk! You are a clever man, and you delight me.'

The discussions with the doctor sitting on the edge of his patient's bed are Ragin's undoing. His rival, the young careerist Khobotov, eavesdrops on them and has his colleague summoned before a medical committee. Ragin is compulsorily retired on the grounds of mental disorder and eventually put in the psychiatric annex along with his former patients. The next day he dies of a stroke.

It would appear that not even this masterly story could induce Akhmatova to take a more tolerant view of Chekhov; six years later she became very agitated when Lydia Chukovskaya praised Chekhov. The clear message of her remark to Berlin, however, seems to me important: if on his return to Oxford Berlin had looked up the text of *Ward No. 6*, he would have found material impossible to talk about freely for two kopeks in a bugged Moscow telephone booth.

In a poem written in 1958 Akhmatova consoles Berlin and herself with the words:

> I do not live in the desert:
> Night and eternal Russia remain with me.

For her the Soviet Union was only a variant of 'eternal Russia' – which was perhaps the chief reason why she did not emigrate. She even read Chekhov's story as a text that could be quite naturally applied to the Communist period.

Chekhov's most important message and statement for and about the year 1956 lies in the central metaphor of his story: the small provincial town, the hospital and the annex, three circles of Hell symbolizing Russia. The town represents society, the health service penal justice. Chekhov's story is full of parallels between hospitals and prisons. The annex is plainly the gulag.

Even the typology of the victims corresponds to the year 1956. The mad Ivan Dmitrich cannot escape his fate whatever happens, while Dr Ragin acts according to the laws of the system until he is ejected from the ranks of the élite through solidarity with the mad patient. Ragin justifies his own inhumanity with the arguments always used by the Russian/Soviet petite bourgeoisie: 'So long as prisons and lunatic asylums exist, they must have people in them. If not you, then myself, if not myself, then someone else.' And when he himself becomes enmeshed in the cogs of the régime, like many Communists of the 1930s, the world becomes unintelligible to him: '"This is some kind of misunderstanding," he said, spreading his arms wide in bewilderment. "The matter must be cleared up, there's a misunderstanding."'

Ivan Dmitrich, on the other hand, represents the outcast, the hostile – not to say dissident – element of society, with his utopian tendencies: '"You can be sure, my good sir, better times will come! You'll laugh if I use a banal expression, but the dawn of a new life will shine, the truth will triumph, then things will be better even for us. I won't experience it, I'll be dead, but our great-grandchildren will experience it.'

By her reference to *Ward No. 6* Akhmatova was trying to convey her view of Soviet history. She respected the suffering of victims who conformed to the system, but above all, she thought of herself as representing *all* those who suffered. In the symbolic context of Chekhov's story this

meant that she identified with the unfortunate Ivan
Dmitrich. By means of Chekhov's description of persecution mania, she could send a personal message. In a previous period of his life Ivan Dmitrich had seen two prisoners
in chains escorted by four soldiers, and strange ideas had
suddenly entered his head.

> He was conscious of no guilt and could vouch for it that
> in future he would never commit murder, arson or theft;
> but surely it wasn't difficult to commit a crime inadvert-
> ently, and were not such things as slander and errors of
> justice possible? . . . In the present legal system an error
> of justice was quite possible, nothing out of the ordinary
> . . . Was it not laughable to think of justice when every
> use of force was greeted by society as a rational and
> expedient necessity, and every merciful act, for example
> an acquittal, gave rise to an outburst of frustrated,
> vengeful feelings?

Conditions of the Russia that Chekhov portrays are
those of 'eternal Russia', and are wholly applicable to the
Soviet era. Even the exact medical description of Ivan
Dmitrich's symptoms carried contemporary resonance:

> Ivan Dmitrich started at every sound or knock on the
> gate of the yard, and was tortured with suspense when
> he came upon anyone he hadn't seen before with the
> landlady; whenever he encountered police, he would
> smile and whistle, so as to appear indifferent. He didn't
> sleep for nights on end, expecting to be arrested, but
> snored and sighed loudly so as to make the landlady
> think he was asleep; for if he did not sleep, it would have
> meant he was suffering the pangs of conscience –
> damning evidence!

In summer 1956, with similar cunning, a great Russian writer advised his British friend to be sure to call from a street call-box if he wished to speak to a person whose telephone was known to be bugged, and this person considered herself equally cunning in murmuring her remark about Chekhov's tale of persecution mania into the receiver as a secret but harmless message in code.

If we are to believe the former KGB officer, Major-General Oleg Kalugin, the Akhmatova file was closed in 1956 by General Mironov, the then head of the Leningrad branch of the KGB. But, curiously enough – indeed, almost inevitably – a secret report has come to light, dated 23 November 1958, summarizing in precise detail Anna Akhmatova's material circumstances and even her mental condition at the time of the Non-Meeting.

Object is in Moscow most of the time, stays there with the Ardov family, spends the summer at the dacha in Komarovo built for her by the Literature Fund, in Leningrad she mostly stays with her adopted daughter Ira Punina-Rubinstein. Very fond of her granddaughter Anya Kaminskaya. Marked physical deterioration: unhealthy corpulence, protruding belly, swollen arms and legs, recurring heart attacks. After the heart attack she sustained in Moscow she has not been able to manage without Validol, but has no telephone at the dacha. Despite everything, her state of mind is fairly cheerful and creative. She has had the idea of writing a book on Paris in 1910 when she met Modigliani there, she has mentioned a desire to publish an autobiographical memoir. The most unpleasant and insulting words that she remembers, and she remembers them with bitterness, are from the CC Resolution, the words attributed to Zhdanov: 'a nun and a whore'. This wounds her greatly. Her attitude to Khrushchev's government is positive, she considers it just and charitable. She often goes to the cemetery one and a half kilometres from her dacha. It's as if she is looking for a place for herself.

5 Late Fame

On 22 June 1959 Aleksey Surkov, Anna Akhmatova's champion and Secretary of the Writers' Union from 1954 to 1959, sent a letter to Nikita Khrushchev, First Secretary of the Central Committee, which included the following passage:

> I consider it my duty to draw your attention to the fate of an old [i.e. pre-revolutionary] Russian writer whose seventieth birthday falls in the second half of June.
>
> I am referring to Anna Andreyevna AKHMATOVA, whose writing was severely criticized in the Central Committee's Resolution on the editorial errors of the journals *Zvezda* and *Leningrad*. Although this criticism was extremely harsh in tone, it was nevertheless correct in content, because the poetess, who together with the entire Soviet people had lived through a period of elevated moral-political uplift during the Great Patriotic War, published a series of deeply pessimistic poems in the first year after the war . . .
>
> The Party's criticism was to leave its mark.

Surkov was clearly referring, in the last sentence quoted, to the infamous cycle of poems entitled *In Praise of Peace* written on the occasion of the fifth anniversary of the end of the Second World War and published in *Ogonyok*; by these 'poems' to the glory of the Motherland (which she later disowned) Akhmatova tried unsuccessfully to obtain her son's release.

In those years her patriotic behaviour was irreproach-
able. While the late M. Zoshchenko, at a meeting with a
group of reactionary English students in Leningrad,
thought he could set the obtrusive visitors against the
Central Committee's Resolution, Anna Akhmatova gave
them a sharp and firm rebuff. A good while before the
hullabaloo last year over the award of the Nobel Prize to
B. Pasternak, I heard Akhmatova herself sharply criticize
the artistic weaknesses and political bias of the novel
Doctor Zhivago, which she had read in a copy of the
manuscript given to her personally by Pasternak.

After these dubious words of praise for Akhmatova,
Surkov came to the point he wished to press:

> Some form of *State* recognition for Anna Akhmatova . . .
> would be a sharp blow to all those reactionaries and
> vacillating intellectuals who are still obsessed by the
> Pasternak Affair.

Anna Akhmatova versus Pasternak – that was the new
trump card with which Surkov planned to put his protégée
in a new league. As a Jesuit among Jesuits he knew very
well the kind of hypocritical logic those in charge of the
system would be most likely to follow. In inner Party
circles elementary justice was still best sold as a thrashing
for the class enemy. The real situation, however, was
simple: Khrushchev was now preparing for his summit
meeting with President Eisenhower. The Soviet Union was
longing to be stroked by the free world once more.

In November 1958 the leadership had won a Pyrrhic
victory. After an unsavoury smear campaign, in which the
Minister for State Security Semichastny had publicly called
Pasternak a pig, the latter's initial resistance had been
broken. Fearing he would be stripped of his citizenship he

declined the Nobel Prize for Literature. The international standing of the Soviet Union had plunged.

In the very week in which Pasternak fell from grace, Akhmatova's volume *Poems* was published in Moscow. Only 25,000 copies of the 131-page book were printed, an absurdly low quantity considering the demand. Known to Akhmatova's friends as 'the Communist Manifesto' because of its red cover, the volume was the product of a double compromise: Surkov's concessions to the official censor were compounded by Akhmatova's forced concessions to Surkov. As a result, a large proportion of the volume was made up of reworkings of Korean, Polish, Romanian and Bulgarian poets, all fruits of Akhmatova's material poverty, not of inspiration. The important thing was that the publication ban that had lasted for fifteen years was now lifted at last. Akhmatova had to exclude many poems old and new, since the tragic events of her life could not be made public. However, the cycle on the Non-Meeting with Isaiah Berlin, of course without mentioning his name, and some fragments of *Poem Without a Hero*, were included.

Akhmatova had welcomed the Swedish Academy's award, congratulating Pasternak personally, despite her strong reservations about *Doctor Zhivago* on aesthetic grounds. About the campaign against Pasternak, which caused her much distress, she made no public statement. To hold this against her, however, would not only be unjust towards the now ageing, ailing and still ostracized poet, but also unhistorical. Public demonstrations of intellectual solidarity, which only a few years previously would have meant certain execution or at least a prison camp sentence, were no longer a feature of Soviet life; those who laid themselves open in this way could only harm themselves, while being of no help to the person they supported.

*

The effectiveness of Surkov's letter, which the General Secretary actually read (judging from file marginalia by his private secretary, Vladimir Lebedev), is unclear. The 22nd Congress of the Communist Party of the Soviet Union, however, had positive results for Akhmatova's career. In October/November 1961 this Congress not only established an exact timetable for the development of Communism, but also confirmed the anti-Stalinist line of the 20th Party Congress. The theses and declarations of Khrushchev's Secret Speech of February 1956 were repeated, but this time out in the open, before the whole Soviet Union. Professed Stalinists were expelled from the Party, and Stalin's body was removed from the Lenin Mausoleum. This ungainly measure – only the building of the Mausoleum was less tasteful – proved a historic watershed: the exhumation of a pharaoh can never be reversed.

Soviet intellectuals expected a national intellectual revival after the Congress, and there were a number of pointers to such a prospect. The young generation of poets gathered around Yevgeny Yevtushenko were allowed to read their poems to large, enthusiastic audiences on public squares and in stadiums around the country. Suddenly, Soviet authors could travel to the West and publish licensed editions of their work. And in November 1962 came the real sensation, when Aleksandr Solzhenitsyn's novella *One Day in the Life of Ivan Denisovich* was published in *Novy Mir*. This breakthrough was due not only to the persistence of the chief editor, Aleksandr Tvardovsky, but also to Vladimir Lebedev, who, bypassing the powerful censorship machinery, had read parts of the manuscript to Khrushchev and persuaded him of the necessity of publication.

The author, a hitherto obscure mathematics teacher, became world-famous overnight. He was the first to treat the subject of the Stalinist Terror openly, legitimizing a Soviet literary genre that in more fortunate countries is the preserve of historians or lovers of the exotic – the discovery of blanks in history.

'Blanks in History' was in fact the title of an essay that the novelist Venyamin Kaverin submitted to *Novy Mir*. In it he attempted to rehabilitate his youthful friend and fellow member of the 1920s literary movement 'The Serapion Brothers', Mikhail Zoshchenko, who had died in 1958. Kaverin evidently thought that after the dethroning of Stalin, his chief ideologue Zhdanov would also become fair game. But he was soon bitterly disappointed. After lying about for months in the editorial department of *Novy Mir*, the manuscript of 'Blanks in History' was returned to its author. The censor Viktor Golovanov was unbending, and indeed wanted to go further still in his banning activities. On 12 December 1962 he wrote in his diary: 'I gave Comrade Semyonova [an employee of the Central Committee's Department of Literature] a selection of Akhmatova's poems; they are unsuitable for publication.' The simultaneous banning of both Zoshchenko and Akhmatova meant that the authorities' fears had a common denominator: the Party Resolution of 1946 was to remain irrevocable.

Anna Akhmatova and her associates harboured the same illusions as Kaverin. In response to Tvardovsky's invitation, Akhmatova submitted a substantial group of poems to *Novy Mir*, which contrary to the title, *From New Poems*, included earlier work. The censor's arguments were ineffective in this instance, and the poems were published in January 1963.

When Aleksandr Tvardovsky had his interview with Khrushchev on 20 October 1962, he complained of difficulties with the censorship over Kaverin's manuscript. He told the First Secretary that in his opinion the Central

Committee's Resolution of 1946 had been overtaken by events, was hopelessly out of date, and that no one dared to invoke it. The ship of Soviet literature, nevertheless, was soon to run aground on this hidden reef.

Khrushchev's reply to Tvardovsky went the rounds of literary circles: 'You can ignore the Resolution of 1946.' Chukovskaya communicated the joyful news to Akhmatova, who said with a heavy sigh: 'What a pity that Mishenka [Zoshchenko] isn't alive to see this!' And she too spread the wonderful story of how Zhdanovism had come to an end.

Paradoxically, even this fairytale contained a kernel of truth. In the early 1960s, in the relatively quiet domain of Soviet encyclopedias, a minor war took place. It has already been suggested that Soviet dictionaries, encyclopedias and reference works of all kinds and levels are not only indispensable handbooks but also clear guides to the increasingly rapid evolution of official thinking. After the 20th Party Congress the editors of the *Great Soviet Encyclopedia* sent a remarkable four-page errata sheet to all subscribers, containing the instruction to remove the article on Beria and stick in a rambling article on the Bering Straits instead.

The editors of the *Little Encyclopedia of Literature* seemed concerned to spare their readers similar trouble, seeking the advice of the highest authority in advance. The urgency of their appeal was related to the alphabet: at the very beginning of their work they were faced with the difficult task of evaluating Anna Akhmatova.

In a letter of 12 February 1962 Aleksey Surkov, chairman of the editorial committee of the publishers of the encyclopedia, and Leonid Shaumyan, Head Expert Adviser, took advantage of the problem to seek to persuade their Party colleagues of the 'necessity of reassessing the work of many Soviet writers in light of the decisions of the

20th and 22nd Congresses of the Communist Party of the Soviet Union'. In the case of Anna Akhmatova and Mikhail Zoshchenko, they considered it 'unsuitable to repeat the sharply negative judgements of the 1946 Resolution in regard to the inadequacies in their work'. The reaction from the highest decision-making body in the Soviet Union was swift and surprisingly positive: loaded terms such as 'un-Soviet', 'tasteless' and 'literary scoundrel' were 'inappropriate' and to be avoided. Of the no less harmful terms 'whore' and 'nun', nothing was said. The historic document was signed by Mikhail Suslov, Boris Ponomaryov, Leonid Ilyichev, Frol Koslov and Aleksandr Shelepin, all Politburo members.

Despite this careful groundwork, the entry on Akhmatova met with little enthusiasm at the highest level. In a report on the 'serious inadequacies' of the first volume of the *Little Encyclopedia of Literature*, dated 18 July 1962, the compilers were reproached in the following terms:

> It is well known how problematic and contradictory the literary career of Anna Akhmatova has been. It has contained many errors and violations. The article devoted to the poetess, however, treats her in an indulgent way, her errors being mentioned *sotto voce* and in a positive tone.

One subject on the agenda of the Central Committee meeting on 31 August 1962 was the report on, or rather against, the *Little Encyclopedia of Literature*. The members of the Committee evidently had little inclination to follow Akhmatova's example and immerse themselves in their own past. The compilers of the encyclopedia were instructed to 'get on with the work without a Central Committee Resolution'. Most of the responsible cultural functionaries still belonged to the Zhdanov School, and their dead chief's hackwork remained sacrosanct to them.

The Resolution of August 1946, however, continued to throw up problems. Two years later the production of the second volume was scheduled, with two impending entries under *Z*, the eighth letter of the Russian alphabet: 'Zoshchenko' and *'Zvezda'*. It would appear that Shaumyan, writing to the Central Committee on 8 October 1964, was anxious to avert another ticking-off: 'in view of the special importance of this question [the Resolution of August 1946], we do not consider ourselves justified in dealing with it without a ruling from the Central Committee of the CPSU. We ask for your instructions.'

Enclosed with this letter was the proposed entry on *Zvezda*, to which Surkov probably contributed, drafted in radical terms:

> *Zvezda* was sharply criticized by the Central Committee's Resolution of 16 August 1946 'On the Journals *Zvezda* and *Leningrad*'. The Resolution rightly urged on the journals the task of increasing the Communist intellectual content of the work they published. At the same time this Resolution, which had been drafted under the direct influence of Stalin, bore the imprint of an administrative relationship to literature and reflected Stalin's pernicious theory of the heightening of the class war in proportion to the advance towards Socialism. The Resolution was coarse in tone and contained unwarrantably severe comments on individual authors.

The bibliographical section of the article omitted all reference to Zhdanov's speech and the Resolution. No one had ever gone quite so far before in applying Khrushchev's criticism of Stalin to the phenomenon of *Zhdanovshchina*.

The middle-ranking leadership of the Central Committee reacted to this article with extreme caution. A letter of 16 October 1964 made no comment at all on the attack on a Central Committee document that was still supposed to retain its validity, but stated laconically: 'We are obliged to recommend to C. [Comrade] Shaumyan that mention of the Resolution of the Central Committee . . . "On the Journals *Zvezda* and *Leningrad*" be removed from the articles on *Zvezda* and Zoshchenko.' For safety's sake the *éminence grise* Mikhail Suslov was informed in writing of this expression of opinion, and he scribbled on the document in his shaky handwriting: 'Agreed. 17.x.64. Suslov.' The timing was not insignificant, for two days before, at a plenum of the Communist Party of the Soviet Union, a new historical era had begun. The unmasker of Stalin, Nikita Sergeyevich Khrushchev, while on holiday in the Crimea, had fallen in a bloodless palace revolution.

If the whole absurdity of the tug-of-war over Akhmatova at this stage of her life is to be fully understood, it should be remembered that during the 'encyclopedia war' unleashed by Surkov the Soviet government had quite other preoccupations. In October 1962 the Cuban Missile Crisis almost led to a third World War. In the following year came the break with China and the splitting of world Communism into two camps, whilst in the summer a catastrophic harvest failure forced the Soviet government to import grain from the United States for gold. Directly or indirectly, Moscow was involved in numerous local conflicts such as the Vietnam War and the Cyprus crisis, and was financing a vast conventional and nuclear armaments programme.

In the cultural domain too, the Party leadership was fully stretched. In order to bring the forces released by the modest liberalization process under control again, two 'meetings between the leaders of the Party and the State and representatives of the artistic intelligentsia' took place in the Kremlin between December 1962 and March 1963; these in fact amounted simply to a large-scale intimidation programme against new nonconformists of various kinds: avant-garde artists, liberal film directors, theatre personnel, writers of memoirs, adherents of modern dancing, especially the twist, which was public enemy number one. But it was all in vain: the Zhdanov Order could not now be reinstated.

Akhmatova had little to do with the encyclopedia war. Her preference was still for 'invisible ink', the language of coded messages. She furnished one poem printed in the January 1963 number of *Novy Mir* with the epigraph: 'You will write about us in your slanting handwriting', giving the source of these words as 'I.B.', thought by some at the time to stand for the Russian prose-writer and Nobel laureate Ivan Bunin (1870–1953), and which I first took, hardly surprisingly, to have been Isaiah Berlin.

However, these initials stood for a young friend of Akhmatova, the poet Joseph Brodsky, whom she had first met in August 1962 when he visited her in Komarovo, bringing her roses, her favourite flowers. He also gave her a belated birthday poem, from which the above-quoted words come. The epigraph and the initials I.B. do not appear in later editions of Akhmatova's poems – at least not under Surkov's editorship. In view of Brodsky's trial, publication ban and later expulsion from the Soviet Union, the well-meaning censor considered his name, even in such indirect form, to be unacceptable.

The German journalist Willi Bongard's visit to Akhmatova in Komarovo, in the company of an interpreter called Rita, must have taken place before mid-September 1962, since

Akhmatova spent most winters with friends in Moscow, and Bongard's article describing the meeting appeared in the Hamburg *Zeit* on 5 February 1963. 'It was curious,' he observed sharply at the beginning, 'that as we approached her dacha, the old lady waved to us from her window, as if she was expecting us. But that wasn't possible – it was only with great difficulty that I had discovered her address on the morning of that very same day.'

It was, in fact, a habit of Anna Akhmatova in old age to stand by the window of her 'cabin' in Komarovo impatiently awaiting the arrival of unannounced guests, in a condition of permanent curiosity, ever ready to meet people and take in new events. 'She liked to know in the morning that someone was coming in the evening,' recalls Margarita Aliger, 'and would not just drop by, but stay for the whole evening – sit with her, drink tea and talk. She got into a nervous state if the phone didn't ring.'

And she recalled one occasion when Akhmatova had been staying with her in Leningrad, and the whole family had had to go away. Aliger didn't want to leave the old lady alone, and was thinking of finding someone to be with her and look after her. Akhmatova, however, assured her hostess that she would be all right by herself. Aliger then left the flat, but forgot something and had to go back, and so by chance heard Akhmatova telephoning from the next room. She was begging one of her young female friends to come at once as she was alone, 'completely alone'. 'She repeated this "completely alone" with such despair,' Margarita Aliger recalls, 'that you could feel how unbearable being on her own was for her.' In her last years Akhmatova scarcely spent a minute alone. Dozens of friends of both sexes were always ready to look after her, help organize her daily affairs, and accompany her everywhere – but she remained chronically lonely.

In old age Akhmatova lived extremely simply, almost in

a state of poverty, although her income from translation work was not inconsiderable. She made no effort to make her living conditions more comfortable or to try to obtain a flat of her own. She would take an almost childish delight in each gift, and then give it to someone else. She did so with the numerous shawls of which she was so fond. Her credo of 1921 seemed to retain a lifelong validity:

> Don't torment your heart with earthly joys,
> Don't cling to your wife or your home,
> Take the bread from your child
> To give to a stranger.

In the same way she always stood by her categorical imperative: 'And don't ask God for anything, ever.'

This undemandingness went with her conviction that in a state system which subjected its citizens to continual threat it was best to possess nothing that could be left behind after arrest. Hers was no dry puritanism – Akhmatova enjoyed food and drink, smoked until her third heart attack of 1961, and loved jokes that were not always decent. Above all, as a counterpart to her deprivations and sufferings, she looked on her own poetry, and everything connected with it, as her highest source of joy. There was only one of her possessions she would have liked to keep safe in a Zurich bank – her battered old trunk from pre-1914 days, in which she preserved her most important manuscripts.

As she grew older and her behaviour in public became less controlled, Akhmatova began to display a characteristic not seen in her before, or at least which she had firmly suppressed: love of self, of her own past and poetry. She admired old photographs of herself, and delighted in poems she found from the Silver Age or articles in Western newspapers in which her name was mentioned. She had an increasing desire for fame, which she had earlier dismissed as 'a plaything of the world'.

A friend, Natalya Ilyina, recalls:

Now, however, Akhmatova began to find consolation in these playthings. She continued to have 'no interest' (her phrase), in material goods. She spent scarcely any time in her new flat in Leningrad, but would stay in Moscow wandering from friend to friend, spending summers in the 'cabin' at Komarovo; she wore an old fur-coat and uncomfortable shoes. But reverence, flattery, deferential admirers of both sexes, flowers and phone calls, with the whole day taken up with visiting and responding to invitations or simply being in company – all this had become necessity for her.

'Fame' came to mean not a volume, thin or thick, with an introduction by Surkov. The poet, the loneliest being in the world, wanted to be embraced by the world. In conversations with friends, the magic words 'Nobel Prize' occurred more and more frequently.

At the same time, Anna Akhmatova was more sensitive than ever, and news from abroad especially could cause her considerable annoyance. When the exiled Russian literary historian Gleb Struve, living in Paris, underestimated the support she had given her son or accused her of 'self-imposed silence' in the 1920s, she was beside herself. The French and Italian versions of her poetry, which were indeed flawed, she felt to be 'inadequate to intolerable' according to Bongard, who described the room where he met her in the following terms:

She received us sitting in the corner on a high chair behind a small writing-table, to the right of the only window lighting a room of peasant simplicity. There was

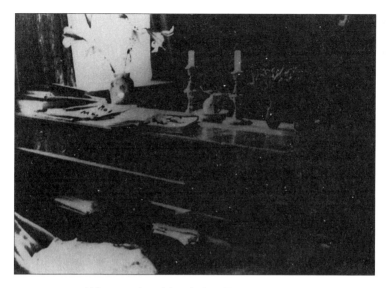

Akhmatova's writing desk at Komarovo, 1960s

a rough wooden bed along one wall, and another made up with coloured blankets along the other. A pair of bookshelves in a corner, not completely filled, an ancient radio and a gramophone on a small table. No cupboards, no carpets; but two icons.

Akhmatova decided to give the visitor a poem. She called to her assistant, a young man in a polo-neck pull-over (the poet Anatoly Nayman, with whom she translated Leopardi and who performed the function of a private secretary), who typed it out. This present, a mono-logue from the drama *Prologue, or Dream within a Dream*, was later published in bilingual text by *Die Zeit*.

    He speaks:
Dear sister of the riverside willows,
Though you are more charming than the angels,

I will murder you with my song,
Not spilling a drop of blood on this earth.
I will not touch you . . .

Akhmatova specialists are generally agreed that '*He*' here is the poeticized figure of the Guest from the Future.

'Akhmatova,' Anatoly Nayman recalls,

always spoke reverently of Berlin, with a thrill of pleasure in her voice . . . she regarded him as an important figure in the West . . . and now he was putting her case for the Nobel Prize, the most distinguished literary prize in the world. When she talked about him she frequently called him, out of ironic respect, 'Lord', and less frequently 'Sir' . . . 'Sir Isaiah, the best conversationist in Europe,' she once said; 'Churchill likes to have him to dinner.'

The Churchill legend gained a good deal of currency, perhaps through Akhmatova herself. 'She has known Isaiah Berlin since 1946,' her friend the literary critic Yury Oksman enthused in his diary, 'he visited her in Leningrad and stayed with her almost till dawn. It turned out that he was an adviser of Churchill at the time.'

Indeed, the linguist Vyacheslav ('Koma') Ivanov, son of the poet, created a wholly new version of the 'Guest from the Future' by demoting him to an accessory: 'Anna Akhmatova told me that when Churchill's son was in Russia, he wanted to meet her. But he couldn't pay her a visit because he was drunk. So he sent a friend.'

While Akhmatova gave her imagination free rein, she was careful to guard her secret from people who did not belong to her most trusted circle. Korney Chukovsky, for example, whom she respected but kept at a distance because of his earlier conformist behaviour towards her, knew next to nothing about the meeting with Isaiah

Berlin. Even when Chukovsky received an honorary doctorate at Oxford in June 1962 at the age of eighty, he still didn't suspect anything; only in the spring of 1965, when Akhmatova was preparing for her trip to Oxford, did the facts of the matter dawn on him.

'Yesterday Anna Akhmatova called,' Chukovsky records in his diary for 27 May 1965.

> I gave her some pretty stupid advice about her coming coronation. Among other things I told her what a wonderful person Sir Isaiah Berlin was, how good and warm-hearted, etc.
>
> And then Lida said to me in passing that A.A. knew Berlin better than I did – that in the 1940s in Leningrad (or Moscow) she had had a romance with him, that many of her poems . . . were dedicated to him, and that he was responsible for her coronation. He is very influential and is of course organizing a sumptuous occasion for her.
>
> But what a long list of conquests she has. She must have plenty to think about at night.

Even during this relatively liberal period there could be no question of regular contact between the two. In London in 1995 my question whether Berlin had ever tried to approach Anna Akhmatova either directly or through an intermediary was answered – in Russian – with a short and categoric 'Never'.

Anatoly Nayman, who perhaps knows more than anyone about Akhmatova's last years, recalls that she gave him a copy of Berlin's essay *The Hedgehog and the Fox* and, after her return from England, a British soldier's hip-flask, which she had received from Berlin. Some of their correspondence between 1956 and 1965 is not extant.

Every now and again there were points of contact. The

Slavist Martin Edward Malia of the University of California, for example, was working for a while in the Moscow archives on the collected works of Alexander Herzen, a subject of special interest to Isaiah Berlin. At the same time Lydia Chukovskaya was engaged in research on the same period, and the intensive conversations between Malia and Chukovskaya soon aroused Akhmatova's curiosity.

'She began to question me about Malia,' Chukovskaya recorded in her diary for 16 November 1962.

> I complained very mildly that he sometimes stayed with me until rather late and I became tired, although it was interesting for me to talk to him . . . 'It isn't surprising that Malia keeps you up,' she said. 'Malia is a friend of Sir Isaiah, and he once stayed with me for twelve hours at a stretch, which was the cause of the Resolution . . .'

More striking, however, were the words of his mentor Berlin that the American quoted direct to Akhmatova: 'Akhmatova and Pasternak have given me back my homeland.' Berlin was referring to the meetings of autumn 1945 which revived his feelings for Russia. 'Flattering, isn't it?' was Akhmatova's response. An unusual degree of emotion may be detected in Berlin's words – 'homeland' alone sounds like an invocation on his lips – which makes Akhmatova's response appear cool in the extreme, for such praise must have been balm to her wounds, offering consolation for all the dreadful experiences which she was convinced were the direct consequences of that single November night in 1945.

Anna Akhmatova was not awarded the Nobel Prize. The Royal Swedish Academy was evidently influenced by the Pasternak scandal. Consideration of the geographical backgrounds of the Nobel laureates over the following years gives the distinct impression that the Academy was following a policy of steering clear of Russia. The Italian Salvatore Quasimodo (1959), the Frenchman Saint-John Perse (1960), the Yugoslav Ivo Andrić (1961), the American John Steinbeck (1962) and the Greek George Seferis (1963) all came from countries with no common border with the Soviet Union. These decisions gave rise to no scandals. Jean-Paul Sartre (1964) was the first to cause a fuss, by declining the Prize. He reproached the Committee for, among other things, having unforgivably ignored Mikhail Sholokhov.

In 1965 the author of *The Quiet Don* was awarded the Nobel Prize – a triumph for the cultural apparatchiks of Moscow. At the 23rd Congress of the Soviet Communist Party scarcely six months later, Sholokhov suggested the appropriateness of the death sentence for Andrey Sinyavsky and Yuly Daniel, who had been sentenced to seven and five years' prison camp respectively for unauthorized publications abroad.

'If these sinister individuals had fallen into our hands in the pioneering '20s,' declared the new Soviet Nobel laureate,

> when we relied on our revolutionary moral consciousness, and were as yet unbound by the restrictive paragraphs of the lawbook, then these wolves in sheep's clothing would have received quite a different punishment! There is room for some reflection when people talk about the 'harshness' of these sentences.

It makes little sense to compare Sholokhov's only genuine novel with Akhmatova's poetry. If, however, she and not he had been awarded the Nobel Prize towards the end of her career, both the Nobel Committee and the Soviet government would have avoided great disgrace.

*

One of the last results of Khrushchev's 'Thaw' was the round table conference of the European Community of Writers (COMES) in August 1963 in Leningrad, at which Akhmatova met the chairman of COMES, Giancarlo Vigorelli. He passed on the news that the following year the town of Catania wished to award her the prestigious Etna-Taormina Prize, and it was probably on this occasion that an invitation to Italy was first discussed.

No one could have been better able to realize such a bold project than Vigorelli. He had succeeded in bringing Sartre to this conference, and also the Hungarian Tibor Déry, who had recently been in prison for his part in the Uprising of 1956. Vigorelli had up his sleeve a tempting proposition for the Soviets – membership of PEN International, an enormous potential prestige-winner for the Soviet Union.

COMES, in Anatoly Nayman's judgement,

> was of pro-Soviet, if not overtly Communist, orientation. At that time the Soviet Writers' Union, under the leadership of Surkov, was in search of honourable possibilities of friendly relations with 'realistically thinking' writers in the West. The Pasternak Affair of five years previously complicated prospects of such a rapprochement, which was desired on both sides. Akhmatova proved . . . an ideal choice for the occasion (*Requiem*, persecution and generally non-Soviet values for them; patriotism and a non-counter-revolutionary attitude for us; high intellectual standing, authority and fame for all).

Vigorelli must have already put out feelers in the summer of 1963, and so when he sent his letter of invitation to Akhmatova in Leningrad he was fairly certain of success. As a practised cultural diplomat he was able to play two strong cards simultaneously – the award of the

Etna-Taormina Prize to Akhmatova and the location of the next conference of the European Community of Writers in Catania, making it possible for Akhmatova to travel to Italy as, so to speak, an official member of the Soviet delegation invited to the conference.

In her first excitement Akhmatova, with the help of friends, sent a letter to Giancarlo Vigorelli in Italian. There is a scarcely concealed euphoria behind the polite, formal phrases – no wonder when it is considered that Akhmatova's last trip abroad had been fifty-two years before. She had long ago given up all hope of seeing the free world. In 1958, when the first delegation of Soviet writers had visited Rome without her, she had expressed her yearning for travel in a melancholy poem:

> All those not expected in Italy
> Send a farewell greeting from the road.
> I remained in my space behind the mirror,
> Where there is neither Rome nor Padua.
> I will not walk the well-known path
> Beneath the sacred and eternal frescoes,
> Nor trade glances secretly
> With Leonardos.

Such melancholy was well-founded. The Soviet superpower guarded its frontiers against its own citizens almost as strictly as against its real or imagined enemies. To visit the West, immense efforts had to be made. Individual tourism in capitalist countries was impossible, group visits were allowed very rarely, and admission to the list of potential members of such groups was a special distinction. Above all, it was impossible to know in advance whether all the trouble of filling in endless forms and obtaining testimonials from superiors at work and the appropriate Party organization would turn out to have been worthwhile. The processing of applications was carried out in the strictest secrecy, and exit visas came through only one or two days before the intended journey. Certain professional trips were the only exception, and some privileged writers – among them Yevtushenko and Voznesensky – were accorded exit visas valid for several trips. All decisions were made by the Foreign Travel Commission of the Central Committee of the Soviet Communist Party, the most important 'expert' role being that of the KGB.

In such conditions it was inconceivable that Akhmatova could have got anywhere near the Etna-Taormina Prize by her own unassisted efforts. Once more Aleksey Surkov intervened on her behalf, this time in none too refined a fashion. First of all, he told his protégée that the Writers' Union had nothing against either the award of the prize to her or the journey to Italy. Only after that, on 25 May 1964, did he write a letter to the Central Committee, in which he explained the composition of the jury. One single member of it, Professor Dibenedetti, was a Communist. Previous laureates had included 'progressive writers' like Umberto Saba, Salvatore Quasimodo and Tristan Tzara. The Prize was worth 1,000,000 Lire (about 2,000 dollars), and this was the first time that a Soviet writer had won it.

Surkov then assessed the career of 'the oldest Soviet writer', who would shortly be seventy-five years old. He did not omit to mention that

> her former husband, N. Gumilyov, was executed for his part in a counter-revolutionary plot, which did not deter her from continuing to live in Russia . . . During the Great Patriotic War she took her rightful place in national life as a Soviet poet, with her patriotic lyric verse and patriotic radio appeals to Leningraders. After the war, when Akhmatova lapsed back into her previous sentiments, her poems were correctly (though in an

extremely harsh tone) criticized in the Resolution of the Central Committee of the Soviet Communist Party on the Journals *Zvezda* and *Leningrad*. This Resolution was not without its effect on Akhmatova . . . new poems of hers began to appear in *Ogonyok* and other journals that restored her to Soviet poetry . . . In all cases when foreign journalists and students tried to provoke Akhmatova to make complaints or anti-Soviet statements, she responded by stoutly rebuffing them, and conducted herself like a worthy Soviet citizen.

In consideration of all the above as well as of the fact that a positive response to the award of the Italian prize to her would be a sharp blow against foreign slanderers, it would be advantageous not to prevent Akhmatova from accepting this prize . . . or from making a two-week trip to Italy to receive it in September/October of the current year, and it would be appropriate to publish information about the award of the prize in *Literaturnaya Gazeta* and *Literaturnaya Rossiya*.

Surkov's deft persuasive powers are evident not only in the way he makes an act of generosity palatable as a 'sharp blow' against the class enemy – reminiscent of his letter to Khrushchev of summer 1959 – but also, or even chiefly, in what he leaves unmentioned. At this time Akhmatova's poetry, including *Requiem* and *Poem Without a Hero*, had already been published in a number of Western countries, in the original and in translation, and the émigré presses that printed original texts did so under the circumspect rubric: 'without the knowledge or permission of the author'. Politically, there was nothing to reproach her with, and the authorities could not very well use the Resolution of August 1946 against her without making themselves appear ridiculous. A ban on her trip to Italy might have produced a wave of indignation in the West –

a 'sharp blow' to Soviet foreign policy, which would scarcely have been able to avoid the charge of inhumanity.

Surkov's carefully constructed argument was successful. V. Snastin and D. Polikarpov of the Ideological Department of the Central Committee contented themselves with giving the chairman of the Writers' Union a gentle rap over the knuckles in a letter of 27 May 1964 to the Politburo: 'It appears from the coded telegram from the Soviet Ambassador in Rome, Com. Kozyrev [father of the future Russian Foreign Minister], that Com. Surkov has given provisional authorization of A. Akhmatova's visit to Italy without obtaining prior agreement on the matter.' There followed a sentence that might be described as 'lacking in ideas' if the phrase were not reserved, in the Communist vocabulary, for the bourgeois-decadent:

> Despite the fact that this Italian literary prize has already been awarded to a number of progressive writers, including Communist writers, its award to A. Akhmatova has a tendentious aspect, constituting as it does support for a poetess whose life's work has been criticized in our country.

For Akhmatova's powerful enemies, therefore – to whose ranks Dmitry Polikarpov had belonged since 1940 – the excommunication of August 1946 still retained some of its force even twenty years later, if now as the sole argument against her.

In the last paragraph of the letter from the Ideological Department one can hear the faint gnashing of teeth:

> Under the circumstances the Ideological Department finds it possible to agree to Com. Surkov's proposal for A.A. Akhmatova's visit to Italy for ten days to receive the

prize and for publication in *Literaturnaya Gazeta* of a short report on the award of the prize to A. Akhmatova.

On 11 June 1964 the demigods of the Politburo, Leonid Brezhnev, Leonid Ilyichev, Pyotr Demichev, Boris Ponomaryov and Mikhail Suslov, added briefly to the mountainous Akhmatova file with their signed expressions of agreement.

Korney Chukovsky, now an old man, noted in his diary: 'Akhmatova to Italy – this is fantastic. She has "not a bone in her body unbroken, / Not a tendon that has not been pulled" [quoting his favourite poet, Nekrasov], and now she's going to Italy to be crowned.' He would have been no Russian writer had he reacted with mere joy to this news. He added grumpily: 'And what about my Zoshchenko article for the *Lit*[*erary*] *Gazette*?' As if there had been any logical connection between Akhmatova's sudden freedom to travel and the freedom to write the truth about a companion in suffering sixteen years after his death, between this chaos of old transgressions still only half-digested by the system and the mistakes that were still to be made by that system.

Akhmatova herself now looked on the trip more sceptically than at the beginning of the project. Shortly before the departure of the train to Rome, she was still racked by suspicion. While her luggage – in borrowed holdalls, as Anatoly Nayman testifies – was being put into her compartment by friends, she stood on the platform in a cold December wind, a long cotton scarf lent to her by Aleksey Tolstoy's widow wound around her, in a state of hesitation. 'I'm going on this trip to represent Communist Russia,' she said, according to Lev Kopelev and Raisa Orlova. To the reassuring words that she was going to represent 'a great power – Russian Poetry', she replied:

'No, my dear friends, I know very well why I am being sent.'

One of those who reported the award of the Etna-Taormina Prize to Akhmatova was the German novelist Hans Werner Richter, founder of the association of left-wing writers Gruppe 47. His broadcast for Freies Berlin and the Norddeutscher Rundfunk on his return from Italy was more in the nature of a prose ode to the general phenomenon of Anna Akhmatova, for he did not know her poetry at all, and at first confused her with the young Bella Akhmadulina.

Giancarlo Vigorelli had prepared a cultural programme for the hundred or so participants in the European Community of Writers' Conference. Pier Paolo Pasolini's new film *The Gospel According to St Matthew* was shown at a cinema in the former monastery of St Domenico. Richter noted meaningfully that Pasolini, who was present at the showing, was 'a Communist and probably a Party member', and at this point launched into a paean of unstinting praise:

> Even if I had known Christ personally, I should still have had to say that I had never seen him more brilliant, more magnetic, more inspiring . . . At the end of the showing there were no atheists left in the cinema. Even the Russians embraced and kissed Pasolini, and one of them had traces of tears in his eyes.

The latter was probably Aleksandr Tvardovsky, chief editor of the liberal literary journal *Novy Mir*. On his return to Moscow he described the film to his colleague Vladimir Lakshin:

> 'The trip was worth it for that alone'; [Tvardovsky] took me through the film for a whole hour. 'To tell you the

truth, I had thought of Christ as an outmoded subject, and did not expect to be moved so much . . . And at the end, when a Russian song was sung – it was somehow out of place but at the same time understandable – I almost burst into tears.'

Akhmatova did not see the film, which she learned about only six months later from Anatoly Nayman when he saw it in an exclusive Moscow cinema, possibly the Kinoteatr Illusion. Nayman's account of the film also had Akhmatova in tears. But turning again to Richter's enthusiastic account:

Ah, Italian Communism, that strange mixture of class warfare, Christianity, socialism, the Catholic Church, tolerance, obstinacy, grandiose gestures and a deep need for social justice, and all this in Sicily . . . in a cinema thick with cigarette smoke. Yes, I almost called out: 'Christus ante portas . . . Christ in front of the gates of Communism . . .'

There are people who maintain that not only a painting or a photograph can be kitsch, but also a real landscape or sunset over the sea. Richter's fascination with socialism in a Sicilian setting was undoubtedly genuine; stifled by Adenauerian Christian-Socialist prosperity, he yearned for a Catholic socialism in Mediterranean conditions. However, what Hans-Werner Richter described so positively, and what was similarly experienced by most of those present, was not reality but autohypnosis induced by the historical moment.

In the early 1960s the Italian Communist Party envisaged the peaceful attainment of socialism in the peninsula by so-called 'structural reforms'. Its attitude towards Soviet and East European models was increasingly crit-

ical. Palmiro Togliatti's posthumous Memorandum, published in *Pravda* in September 1964, held out the bur-
geoning hope of Western Communism contributing to
democratization in the East. This illusion, however, was
not to last very long.

Neither did the remarkable international solidarity of
writers in Catania, where the Soviet delegation basked
with their brothers in the warmth generated by their formerly ostracized compatriot. It was not long before Soviet
writers, who had so recently become socially acceptable,
were competing with each other in their condemnation of
Aleksandr Solzhenitsyn, congratulating the Party leadership on the occupation of Czechoslovakia, and conspiring
with the censorship to hound Tvardovsky from the editorship of *Novy Mir*; while the same Soviet literary community
managed to withhold any mention of the complete political and moral rehabilitation of its Etna-Taormina laureate
until 1988.

Tired after her long journey, Akhmatova had excused
herself from attending the performance of Pasolini's film,
and she was spared attendance at the conference for the
same reason. She was accompanied by Nikolay Punin's
daughter Irina – a last-minute arrangement made when
her close friend the actress Nina Ardova, who was originally due to go with her, suffered a heart attack in
September.

The award ceremony was shortened because of
Akhmatova's poor state of health. In view of the occasion,
she read 'The Muse', written in 1924:

When at night I await her coming,
It seems that life hangs by a strand.
What are honours, what is youth, what is freedom,
Compared to that dear guest with rustic pipe in hand.

And she entered. Drawing aside her shawl
She gazed attentively at me.
I said to her: 'Was it you who dictated to Dante
The pages of *The Inferno*?' She replied: 'It was I.'

'Yes, she read in Russian,' reported Richter,

> in a voice that sounded like a distant thunderstorm,
> whether approaching or receding was never clear. Her
> dark, rolling tones contained no bright notes. The first
> poem she read was short, very short, and was greeted as
> soon as it was ended by a storm of applause, although,
> apart from the Russians present, no one understood
> Russian . . . The occasion resembled . . . some New Year
> reception at an empress's court. A tsarina of poetry was
> receiving the homage of the diplomatic corps of world
> literature . . . [After the ceremony] word reached us that
> she was tired, and then out she walked, a tall woman,
> taller by a head than all the poets around her, a statu-
> esque figure against which the waves of time had
> broken from 1889 until today, and so when I saw her
> come out I suddenly understood why Russia can some-
> times be ruled by tsarinas . . .
>
> Only one of them [the Russians] said anything critical,
> but I won't name him, to spare him Anna Akhmatova's
> indignation. He said, after I had kissed her hand in fare-
> well in the style of my country: 'You know, in 1905, at
> the time of the first Russian revolution, she was a very
> beautiful woman.'

Lev Kopelev, a new friend of Akhmatova, told me that
as soon as he obtained the text of Richter's rapturous
report he went to Akhmatova with it and translated it for
her, omitting the words just quoted. However, he care-
lessly left the magazine with Akhmatova. Speaking to him

on the telephone she said: 'Lev Zinovevich, you are a real gentleman. And now translate the whole text for me. But please with no omissions.'

In referring both to her international fame and what she took to be Berlin's representations on her behalf, Anna Akhmatova often employed the same term, *khlopoty*, that she had used when speaking of her own campaign to obtain Lev's release. She saw a late fame coming to her and envisaged its high-point in her approaching death:

> Dawn breaks – it's the Last Judgement.
> Meeting is more bitter than parting.
> There your living hands
> Hand me over to posthumous fame.

Akhmatova gave this four-liner the unusually elaborate title 'From the Diary of a Journey: an occasional poem'. It is dated 'December 1964' in all editions. The context could only have been the Catania trip, and the occasion of inspiration during this trip was probably connected with the mythical figure of the Guest from the Future, who in Akhmatova's mind was 'responsible' for the Etna-Taormina award.

In a letter dated 20 October 1964 to Joseph Brodsky in exile near Arkhangelsk, Akhmatova wrote:

> Joseph,
> from the endless conversations that I have had with you day and night, you will know everything that has happened and not happened.
> What has happened:
>
> 'Fame's high threshold
> Is here already,

> But a cunning voice
> Forewarned me:' etc.

What has not happened:

'Dawn breaks – it's the Last Judgement' etc.

The first quotation is from the long poem *The Way of All the Earth* (1940) and refers to the first phase of Akhmatova's post-revolutionary fame, with the publication of her selection *From Six Books*, acceptance as a member of the Writers' Union, and the attempt made by a number of colleagues to propose her for the Stalin Prize. That is 'what happened', and what ended with the banning of the new volume. Her post-war fame was equally short-lived. Akhmatova always had to pay for her fame, and often at a very high price – in the 1940s with excommunication, and in the 1960s, so it seemed to her, with her own life.

In Akhmatova's view it had been appropriate for great Russian poets since Pushkin to fall out of favour. When in spring 1963 Joseph Brodsky was found guilty of 'parasitism' by a Leningrad court, Akhmatova made a good deal of *khlopoty* on his behalf. At the same time she found inspiration in his fate: 'What a biography is being prepared for our red-head! As if he'd had this done on purpose!'

It was in this light that Akhmatova began increasingly to remind Anatoly Nayman, with whom she was translating some poems by Leopardi, that her days were numbered. She regarded her own death as not so much biologically inevitable as the dark companion of inevitable fame. In other words, an immortal has to die first.

Had there been such a connection between the growth of fame and the approach of death in the real world and not just in Anna Akhmatova's imagination, nurtured on Oscar Wilde's *Dorian Gray*, the Soviet cultural authorities would have been in no way responsible for her death. They had never spoilt her, had celebrated neither her seventieth nor her seventy-fifth birthday, and had taken only a few tentative steps to accord her a measure of respect. Ignaty Ivanovsky has described how, after the operation on her appendix and the heart attack that followed, a representative of the local Writers' Union appeared at her bedside in a Leningrad hospital with a bunch of flowers and offered to have her moved to a better hospital. Akhmatova is said to have replied: 'No thank you. I've already been cut in half.'

The only event that can be interpreted as a sign of official approval was the decision in March 1965 to elect her to the presidium at the 2nd Congress of the Union of Writers of the Russian Republic (RSFSR). This decision, however, was far from an answer to the rhetorical question put in the foreword of the French edition of her poetry: 'When will the Soviet Union realize that it should be just as proud of Akhmatova as of Gagarin and Titov?'

The last great recognition came from quite another direction: on 15 December 1964 the University of Oxford decided to confer a Doctorate of Letters, *honoris causa*, on Anna Akhmatova.

6 *Honoris causa*

On 27 October 1964, in reply to a telephone enquiry, Isaiah Berlin wrote to Maurice Bowra giving Akhmatova's address: Ulitsa Lenina 42, flat 23, Leningrad.

> It will, I think, be best to send her both a telegram and a formal letter, saying in the telegram that a letter follows and that therefore no immediate answer from her is expected – otherwise she may panic about the possibility of visas, etc.

Berlin suggested sending a copy of the telegram and the letter via the diplomatic bag to the British ambassador in Moscow, with copies also to the Soviet ambassador in London and

> to dear Miss Brenda Tripp of the British Council, whose feelings towards Akhmatova are very tender and whom I can tip off about the possibility of this anyway – she could be asked in a covering letter to inform the Foreign Office or any other institutions in England that may be desirable (e.g. Great Britain–USSR Society . . .): I think that completes the formalities.

Those behind the award already knew of Akhmatova's forthcoming trip to Italy, from which they concluded that a further trip to Britain might be perfectly possible for her. On 3 November they sent an official telegram to Leningrad: 'The University of Oxford invites you to accept an honorary degree of Doctor of Letters', ending with the reassuring words: 'No need to reply to telegram'. The letter sent on the same day signed by the University Registrar, Sir Folliot Sandford, was also reassuring: 'there would be no difficulty in arranging a special degree ceremony at a date when you were in this country.'

Meanwhile Brenda Tripp, now head of the East European Section of the British Council, possessed of a deep knowledge of Soviet institutions and also of Anna Akhmatova herself, had swung into action. She had been present in November 1945 when Berlin had set off for Fountain House from the Writers' Bookshop, and had been working in Moscow at the time of Akhmatova's excommunication. She was well aware how delicate the present task was – a poet only half-way towards official recognition was being invited to an English university that counted among its leading figures none other than Isaiah Berlin, son of a Russian émigré, a former diplomat who, like other foreigners at the time, had once been regarded as a possible spy. Behind the confidential corres-pondence between different institutions – the Foreign Office department dealing with East–West relations soon became involved as well – an intrigue was being hatched on behalf of an elderly lady from whom at first nothing was heard.

The parties involved seem to have informally agreed that the British Council was the most appropriate body to take a lead in handling the project. The Council had a legitimate Soviet counterpart, the State Committee for Cultural Relations with Foreign Countries. The reactions of the Soviet authorities could be ascertained through diplomatic channels. In order to complete the necessary preparations for the ceremony, a positive signal was needed in Oxford by the end of November at the latest.

At last, on 1 December, in the middle of preparations for

her trip to Italy, Anna Akhmatova sent a telegram from Moscow saying she accepted the honour to be conferred on her 'with gratitude'. Over the date of her visit she was more cautious: 'it depends on the state of my health'. She clearly had in mind not only her blood pressure and the state of her heart, but also the official response to her invitation.

Only after this lengthy preamble did Oxford University, on 15 December, decide to make Akhmatova's forth-coming honour public. On the following day all the leading British newspapers reported it – putting polite pressure on Moscow. The Soviet authorities could not simply dismiss the invitation as provocation, for at almost the same time, at Surkov's instigation, *Literaturnaya Gazeta* carried the shortest of news items announcing the award of the Etna-Taormina Prize to Akhmatova, proof that Soviet cultural policy-makers considered the poet – 'in principle', as Radio Yerevan would have said – able to travel.

On 16 December 1964 the Director-General of the British Council, Sir Paul Sinker, sent an official letter to Akhmatova containing one sentence addressed not to her but to the authorities of her country: 'We send you this invitation in accordance with the appropriate article of the Anglo-Soviet Inter-governmental Agreement signed in London in January 1963.'

Sir Paul's letter of invitation presumably went round a number of different organizations and departments before reaching its addressee. Not until 21 February 1965 was Akhmatova able to write to Aleksey Surkov:

In view of the fact that I have accepted Oxford University's award of an honorary Doctorate in Literature, it is obligatory for me to be personally present in Oxford.

Could you please prepare travel documents for me
and for Kaminskaya, Anna Genrikhovna (born in 1939),
daughter of my step-daughter, who will go with me,
since I cannot travel alone because of my state of health.

Anna Akhmatova
21 February 1965

She did her best to make things easy for the decision-
makers by telling the correspondent for the *Oxford Mail*
sent to interview her in Leningrad: 'I have no disagreements with the Writers' Union now. The poems just published have been selected by myself and represent all I
want to have published for the present.' As we have seen,
this was not actually the case with the last book of poems,
The Flight of Time, published in her lifetime.

Despite this apparently auspicious beginning, the execution of Akhmatova's request proceeded at a snail's pace.
When enquiries arrived from Oxford as to Anna
Akhmatova's size for the preparation of her doctoral gown
and hat, a date for the award ceremony could still not be
fixed. To do so was particularly urgent for the university
because three other candidates, the Italian literary critic
Gianfranco Contini, the English poet Siegfried Sassoon,
and the British surgeon, bibliographer and editor of
William Blake, Sir Geoffrey Keynes, were to be similarly
honoured on the same day.

In mid-March the University Vice-Chancellor's office
asked the Foreign Office to try to hasten proceedings in
Moscow. The Foreign Office entrusted the task to the
British cultural attaché in Moscow, who again reminded
Britain's partner in the cultural agreement of 1963 of its
obligation under Article XI of that agreement. This pressure was successful. On 29 March Akhmatova herself
informed the university authorities that she would come

after 1 June. On 7 April a date was at last fixed: the cere-mony would take place on 5 June at half-past two.

The British side took concrete measures. On 3 May Isaiah Berlin invited Anna Akhmatova and Anya Kaminskaya to stay at his house in Headington from 1 to 6 June; after that, relatives from the United States were to stay with him. Two rooms were booked at the President Hotel in Russell Square, London for 29 May, Akhmatova's planned day of arrival.

As we know today from Soviet secret documents, it was only at this stage that the Moscow authorities managed to cut through the complexities of the hierarchical jungle and reach a final decision. On 22 May Demichev, a Politburo member, and Nikolay Podgorny, Chairman of the Presidium of the Supreme Soviet and head of state, set their signatures to the application from the Writers' Union, which already bore that of Akhmatova's arch-enemy Polikarpov. The foreign travel committee not, this time, of the Central Committee but 'only' of the Leningrad Regional Party Committee, authorized Akhmatova's two-week trip at its meeting on 24 May. The relevant 'excerpt from the minutes' of this meeting was sent on Thursday 27 May to the Passport Office. Then came a weekend, and the travel papers and tickets were finally issued to Akhmatova by the Writers' Union on Monday 31 May, which was now supposed to be the day of her departure.

Akhmatova wanted to get to London as soon as possible. In view of her heart condition, however, the doctors advised against air travel. The train journey from Moscow via Warsaw, Cologne and Ostend lasted over forty hours. What stress her fragile heart had to endure during this time may be imagined from eyewitness accounts. Korney Chukovsky, himself awarded an honorary degree at Oxford three years previously, recorded his observations of Akhmatova's preparations for her trip in his diary:

16 May 1965 . . . Akhmatova is getting ready for her trip to England. She is coming to see me. Her coronation takes place in June . . .

28 May. Anna Akhmatova hasn't yet left for England. Our people haven't yet issued her visa. She is sitting on her packing-cases at the Ardovs' . . .

31 May . . . First they told Akhmatova she was travelling on Friday, then on Tuesday, but her visa wasn't issued until Monday.

Anatoly Nayman, describing the tug-of-war over Akhmatova's visa, records the seventy-six-year-old's agonizing during her days of waiting: 'What are they thinking? That I won't come back? That I've stayed behind here, when everyone else has left the country, that I've lived my whole life – and what a life! – in this country, just so that I can now go and live somewhere else?' The idea that behind the prevaricating and obstructionism of the authorities there lay any kind of rational thinking was one of the many fantasies of powerlessness cherished by Soviet citizens, who were always trying to 'think with THEIR minds'.

On the eve of her trip to Oxford, there was one significant matter regarding Akhmatova still unresolved. The Central Committee's Department for Agitation and Propaganda was frequently concerned at this time with works by Soviet writers that had reached the West 'by illegal routes', and 'contained slanders against the Soviet Communist Party and represented our life and the domestic and foreign policy of the Soviet state to the Western reader in a distorted form'. As well as works by Solzhenitsyn, Okudzhava, Brodsky and others, there was 'a cycle of poems not published in our country often referred to by the title "Requiem", ascribed to A. Akhmatova'. Against the background of the arrest of

Andrey Sinyavsky and Yuly Daniel already being planned, such accusations were no joke. For the moment, however, the Department for Agitation and Propaganda confined itself to asking the KGB simply to identify the authors of such blacklisted publications.

The prevarication over arrangements for Akhmatova's already sanctioned trip was, therefore, not a punishment, but simply what Hamlet calls 'the proud man's contumely'. Whereas she had been given almost four months to make her travel preparations after the Politburo had given its approval of the award of the Etna-Taormina Prize, she now had to undertake this task, a demanding one for someone of her age and state of health, in a mere few days. Middle-ranking officials, probably irritated by liberalism at the highest levels of the state apparatus, did all they could to remind the favoured poet of her continuing helplessness by working to rule. That newspapers like *The Times* and the *Daily Telegraph* were announcing the arrival in Britain of the 'Matriarch of Russia's poets', 'the Russian Sappho', in their headlines, did not appear to have the slightest influence on how matters proceeded in Russia. What was a Sappho to the apparatchiks? They would have tried to teach a Sophocles, a Dante or a Goethe about human rights.

In this case, however, the Soviet apparat put a spanner in its own works. When Anna Akhmatova arrived at Victoria Station late in the evening of Wednesday 2 June, waiting to meet her were not only British Council officials and numerous journalists but also the Soviet Cultural Attaché, Vsevolod Sopinsky. The latter was concerned. 'If an invitation arrives tomorrow,' he was reported by the *Daily Telegraph* as saying, 'it will be too late.' What he meant was that if the Soviet Embassy in London did not receive an invitation to the award ceremony until the following day, Thursday 3 June, attendance by official representatives of the Soviet Union could not be assured. Soviet diplomats were restricted to a 30-mile radius of London unless they had special Foreign Office permission, and for this three working days' notice was required.

Utter astonishment that they had not been invited to the award ceremony at Oxford on Saturday 5 June was the official reaction of the representatives of a state that had agreed to this visit by its greatest living poet only with the greatest reluctance. A spokesman for Oxford University explained that no snub had been intended to Soviet Embassy officials; recipients of Oxford honorary degrees were always asked whom they would like to be invited to the ceremony, and this would have been done in the present case. Akhmatova's hosts would appear to have been unaware of or to have overlooked the fact that it was entirely at variance with Soviet practice for an ordinary citizen to issue an invitation to an official personage on any occasion whatsoever.

'Anna Akhmatova, Andreae filia,' as the laureate was referred to in the University Orator's address in Latin in the Sheldonian Theatre, wearing her red ermine-lined gown and black doctoral hat, was presented as 'a poetess of the highest distinction' – 'femina haec augusta' – 'most justly called by some critics the Russian Sappho'. Her most important works were listed, her patriotic achievements during the Second World War were mentioned, but her persecution by the authorities of her country was not. 'Some years after the restoration of peace' – the cautious dating indicates some uncertainty over the details of her career – 'she made an anthology of two hundred and fifty poems, and this was printed by the State Publishing House.'

The official translation of the Orator's address issued by the Foreign Section of the Union of Soviet Writers refers,

Akhmatova with Anna Kaminskaya (left) *in Oxford, 5 June 1965, after the award of her honorary D.Litt.*

astonishingly, to 'two hundred and twenty poems', and makes an extraordinary further mistake: the title of the early poem 'By the Very Sea' is mistranslated from the English text of the address as 'By the Very Bluest Sea'. Anyone who lived in Russia and listened to the radio at that time will know that these were the opening words of a hit song. And the 'anthology', incidentally, must be the 'Anthology of Korean Verse' translated by Anna Akhmatova, which was published in two editions in 1956 and 1958.

Akhmatova's last foreign trip consisted of ten days in England supplemented by a visit to Paris. There is little detailed record as to how she spent her time in Oxford, though we know in general whom she talked to. In an interview with *The Times* she chose to mention only Maria Petrovykh among contemporary Russian poets. In her Oxford hotel room she recorded several of her own poems, including *Requiem*, for her hosts. In the course of her visit she held extended conversations with some fifty people. Friends from her youth, former lovers, Russian journalists in exile and relatives whom she hadn't seen for fifty years – all contributed to an atmosphere in which Akhmatova was able to pass her life in review.

At seventy-six years of age, Anna Akhmatova was clearly physically and mentally overtaxed by this second triumphal visit outside her own country. Her two companions, Anya Kaminskaya and the young Amanda Haight, future author of the first biography of the poet, had to monitor her powers of endurance at all times and be firm with enthusiastic, nostalgic or simply curious vistors. With the help of Kaminskaya, the actor Vladimir Retsepter later attempted to reconstruct Akhmatova's daily programme, from which the following brief extracts are quoted.

3 June . . . Akhmatova's name in headlines in London newspapers, some calling her 'The Russian Sappho' . . . Mountains of flowers in her hotel room – dark-red roses . . .
4 June. Akhmatova makes a tour of London. In the evening, to Oxford by car; caught in a traffic jam.

5 June, morning. Formal breakfast at Oxford University. The award ceremony . . .

Then two days at Stratford on the Shakespeare circuit. At Shakespeare's birthplace Anna Akhmatova stays in the car. She feels unwell . . .

Anya also visits Anne Hathaway's cottage without Akhmatova, who waits in the car . . .

The evening of the next day has been planned as the climax of the excursion to Stratford – a production of *The Merchant of Venice* at the Memorial Theatre . . . Akhmatova, fearing that her knowledge of English will be inadequate for her enjoyment of the performance, went to the Russian bookshop while in London and bought volume three of the eight-volume Russian edition of Shakespeare containing *The Merchant of Venice*, 'Venetsianskiy kupets', translated by T. Shchepkina-Kupernik.

On the evening before the performance Akhmatova and Kaminskaya read the play together in their hotel.

. . . When the time comes to go to the theatre . . . Akhmatova feels worse than yesterday. She is unable to leave the hotel.

Anya is afraid to leave her alone, but Akhmatova insists on her going to the theatre: 'This will be an experience that will last you a lifetime . . .'

*

Akhmatova was stirred by many questions raised by English journalists and even more by exiled Russian friends in Paris; almost everyone who talked to her wanted to hear her opinion of the Soviet poets of the New Generation, by which they understood almost exclusively Yevgeny Yevtushenko and Andrey Voznesensky. What was new about these poets was that they managed to combine explosive political and private subjects with a large dose of individuality. They carried echoes of the 1920s – the work of the politically minded Yevtushenko was reminiscent of Mayakovsky, while that of Andrey Voznesensky, a trained architect, seemed to have links with the Formalists.

At the end of the 1950s and beginning of the 1960s, the New Generation expressed a mood of anti-Stalinist Storm and Stress. Their books of verse were published in editions of tens of thousands, and thousands came to the readings on Mayakovsky Square and in stadiums elsewhere; these poets became leading national figures. Despite their criticism of the conditions of Soviet life, they retained the essential mentality of Soviet society, the root cause of their phenomenal rise and ultimate failure. Even at the height of their cultural power, there was something semi-official and ambiguous about their status. They enjoyed a relatively generous freedom of travel and regularly published poems about experiences that most of their readers could not even dream of. They increasingly became articles of export – as the dissident Andrey Amalrik later put it, 'the red caviare of Soviet cultural politics'.

When Anna Akhmatova was confronted, during this visit to the West, with the wildly popular presence of the New Generation – Voznesensky also visited England in the summer of 1965 and sent her a telegram of greeting – the movement's standing in Russia had already declined. After Khrushchev's public outbursts of anger towards 'heretics' in literature and the arts in December 1962 and March 1963, the leading representatives of the New Poetry had been exercising humble self-criticism. This was an indication that the radical critical potential of the 'new' generation was already exhausted – as an artistic credo, social commitment as prescribed by the 20th Party Congress of the Soviet Communist Party was not enough to sustain a lifetime's work. It was primarily in the West that these no longer young figures managed to retain the reputation of being the leading rebels of Soviet writing, the Moscow 'Beat Generation'.

The New Generation created a situation for Akhmatova that was similar to one she had experienced already. In the 1920s, so she wrote to Anatoly Nayman in January 1960, she had been marginalized in literary life by what is presumed to have been an official publication ban in 1925. At that time the younger generation only wanted great Revolutionary poetry. 'All the other poets were avant-garde, newer and more fashionable than me: Mayakovsky, Pasternak, Tsvetayeva. I won't say anything about Khlebnikov – he was an innovator *par excellence*.'

The situation with the New Generation was not dissimilar. The younger poets, whose education and technical abilities did not equip them to hold a candle to Akhmatova, simply struck the public as 'more interesting'. Akhmatova's poem 'To the Defenders of Stalin' was written at around the same time as Yevtushenko's 'The Heirs of Stalin' (October 1962). While Yevtushenko's topically inspired text found its way straight from the typewriter into the next edition of *Pravda*, Akhmatova's sombre, prophetic lines were not published until 1989.

In other words, during her most productive period Anna Akhmatova was out of step with her time. She was most in tune with the immediate post-war years; it was no accident that this was her brief moment of triumph. She did not really belong in the post-1956 period, despite the relief it brought her in many respects. Her anti-Stalinism was more personal than political; her pain and anger were at once timeless and specific to her time. How would Antigone have pleaded for her brother's right to due burial before the central organ of a one-party state?

Her poetry, furthermore, makes for wonderful but not agreeable reading. Her major masterpiece, *Poem Without a*

Hero, is extremely difficult to assimilate – almost every line presupposes a thorough cultural grounding in the Russia of the first decade of the twentieth century, and the 'invisible ink', the 'mirror writing', sets the reader a good deal to do.

The form of great poetry often survives its content. What keeps *Poem Without a Hero* alive, for example, although it belongs to a past age, is the precision of its imagery and the instantly recognizable solemn, tragic music of the Akhmatovan stanza. The first lines of the poem, after the three Dedications,

> From the year nineteen-forty
> I look down as from a tower

will suggest as exact a sense of period to future generations of Russian readers as the opening stanza of *The Divine Comedy* to Italians or of Heine's *Deutschland* to Germans. Today the two last-mentioned poems can no longer be appreciated without footnotes. Only a few years after the long poems of most contemporaries of Dante, Heine and Akhmatova were written, however, no footnotes could be of any further help to them.

In June 1965 Berlin asked Akhmatova if she would ever annotate *Poem Without a Hero* since 'the allusions might be unintelligible to those who did not know the life it was concerned with'.

She answered that when those who knew the world about which she spoke were overtaken by senility or death, the poem would die too; it would be buried with her and her century; it was not written for eternity, nor even for posterity: the past alone had significance for poets – childhood most of all . . . Vaticination, odes to the

future . . . were a form of declamatory rhetoric, a striking of grandiose attitudes, the poet's eye peering into a
dimly discernible future, a pose which she despised.

But beside such statements the defiantly hopeful sentence 'But my voice will still be recognized' is one of many
hints that Akhmatova desired and expected immortality
and the admiration of posterity. To her, the poem *Requiem*
not only commemorated the victims of the Great Terror
but also immortalized her own human and poetic achievement. For through her own 'tortured mouth' 'one
hundred million people cry', and that made her certain
that 'a memorial in this country' would be dedicated to
her. She stood in the tradition of Pushkin, who in his poem
with the Horatian epigraph 'Exegi monumentum' thus
founded his claim to immortality:

> Because in our harsh age I sang of Liberty,
> Because my lyre awakened noble sentiments
> And, for the fallen, Charity.

At the time of writing, Berlin's is the only published
account we have of Akhmatova's conversations with him
in Oxford. It may be that the next volume of Lydia
Chukovskaya's *Akhmatova Journals* will contain some 'personal impressions' on Akhmatova's side.* Anatoly Nayman
quotes a comment she made about Berlin:

> After her return from England, she described meeting a
> person who occupied a special place in her life. Now he
> lived, according to her description, in a splendid house,
> surrounded with flowerbeds; he had servants and silver.

* Published by Soglasiye, Moscow, 1997. An English edition is currently
in preparation. – *Translator.*

'It seemed to me,' she said, 'that a man should not shut himself up in a gilded cage.'

This light reproof is to some extent to be ascribed to the culture shock of a Soviet citizen on being introduced to Western material standards. Korney Chukovsky, on his visit to Oxford, was greatly struck by the affluence of academic circles, the 'top ten thousand'. Berlin's wife, 'a millionaire's granddaughter', made a particular impact on him.

> Lady Berlin . . . a graceful, quiet, extraordinarily sensitive woman, led me to her son's room, an enormous room, half of which was occupied by a (toy) railway system, with stations and so on. Surrounded by crude-looking but harmless comics, the boy was watching television (African jungle scenes). On the table lay a Latin grammar; I asked him the conjugation of the different forms of verbs, and on this and Latin declensions he gave faultless answers . . . I forgot to mention that Shostakovich stayed at the Berlins' house when he was awarded an honorary doctorate.

The perpetually homeless Akhmatova could find little enthusiasm for this family idyll, and her conversations with Lady Berlin, despite the latter's charm, remained cool and formal. Her remark about the 'gilded cage' certainly did not apply to the latter; it has a context of its own. The image appears again in one of Akhmatova's last poems, of four lines, dated 5 August 1965:

> Not to a secret pavilion
> Does this flaming bridge lead:
> Him to a cage of gold,
> And her to a red scaffold.

The flaming bridge is the path to fame. But the way divides into two: one, the man's, leading to confinement, weighed down by honours and achievements, in a gilded cage, and the other, the woman's, to death. Now that the destiny that brought the two together is fulfilled, their ways part.

The fear of fame is also found in another verse fragment, likewise written in 1965:

> Pray, at night, that you won't
> Awake to sudden fame.

These lines point to the evil awakening of August 1946, when the anathema pronounced by Zhdanov made Akhmatova a national name overnight.

> *On your account* I had to pay with blood money,
> Ten years I lived my life under the gun . . .

she complains to the Guest from the Future of this time of 'ill repute', which constantly 'rustles' behind her, throwing a disproportionate shadow over the 'good repute' she thought of as compensatory. This process was more than symbolic. On her return from Italy the previous year, Akhmatova told Berlin in Headington, KGB men had asked her for her impressions of Rome: 'had she come across anti-Soviet attitudes on the part of writers, had she met Russian émigrés? . . . What would she answer when similar questions were put to her, as they inevitably would be, about England? London? Oxford?'

These fears explain at least in part why Akhmatova's meeting with Berlin in June 1965 contained more sadness than the years between 1946 and 1956 or the 'Non-Meeting' of August 1956. Akhmatova had always had fears, and she had learned to live with them and to fight against them. In June 1965, however, her zest for life had gone. The last meeting in Oxford was permeated with a profound melancholy reminiscent of *Lotte in Weimar*.

Unlike the tenant in Fountain House, the woman who saw Isaiah Berlin again in Oxford was already looking towards death.

> O Lord! Don't you see I'm tired
> Of resurrecting, dying and living

she had written in 1962, in the poem 'Last Rose' dedicated to Joseph Brodsky. She had hardly any plans for the future, and when she said good-bye to her many friends old and new in England and France, she said 'Au revoir' out of politeness rather than conviction. Twenty years on, the visit by the Guest from the Future had been reciprocated by a 'guest from the past'.

7 *Earthly and Heavenly Justice*

Anna Akhmatova's undying greatness caused no small problems for posterity. Shortly after her death a legal contest ensued between the Punin family and her son Lev over her literary archive. Akhmatova had originally wished to leave the whole of her estate to the archive of the Institute of Russian Literature (Pushkin House), Leningrad, in order, as she said, to bring her 'eternal romance' with Pushkin to a posthumous conclusion. Lev, the Punin family and Akhmatova's closest friends are supposed to have agreed to this when they met together after the funeral. Lev asked a token sum of one hundred roubles from Pushkin House for the archive, which contained a large number of original manuscripts possessing a high commercial value after the recent death of their author.

The legendary trunk containing Akhmatova's manuscripts, however, from which she had never been parted during her lifetime, was in the Punins' flat. When Irina Punina and her daughter Anna Kaminskaya divided up the archive and sold it to the Saltykov-Shchedrin Library, Leningrad, and the Central Archive of Literature and Art, Moscow, Lev Gumilyov and Pushkin House tried to stop the sale. The case lasted four years, after which a court of the Leningrad City District of Zhdanov found in favour of the Punin family.

Some, including the poet Joseph Brodsky, have seen the influence of the KGB behind this outcome, aiming to prevent embarrassing details of the conflict between Akhmatova and national cultural policy-makers from surfacing in public. To date, however, there has been no direct evidence of collusion between the Punin family and the literati of the Lubyanka. The fact remains that because of the poor state of the source material, the life and work of Anna Akhmatova, despite the opening of the archives, remains one of the most daunting areas of recent Russian literary history.

The Party tolerated Akhmatova's late fame, which had found especial focus in the Etna-Taormina and Oxford awards, and sought to make capital out of her world-wide celebrity. Ten years after her death, the most complete critical edition of her poetry appeared, again with a fore-word by her champion Aleksey Surkov in which, despite his veneration of her work, he did not fail to make brief, if non-committal, mention of the Resolution of 1946. Conscientious footnotes compiled by the literary historian Viktor Zhirmunsky, who had died by the time the edition was published, were equally devoid of references to the dramatic conflicts of Akhmatova's life – the execution of her first husband, the arrest of her second, and the prison camp sentences of her son. Zhdanov's speech of August 1946 went unmentioned. Almost all the poems involving Berlin were included, but no reference to his name appeared. And of course *Requiem*, Akhmatova's lyrical reckoning with the Great Terror of the 1930s, was excluded.

Even official recognition of this kind, however, contained elements of canonization and split the community of Akhmatova's readers. On one side stood those who wished to see her received as a domesticized classic of Soviet culture, either from a genuine enthusiasm for her poetry or because they were following the line of least resistance. Akhmatova was cited with increasing frequency, and a stream of reminiscences by contemporaries appeared in literary journals. Some of these contained new and interesting information, but overall, because they respected existing taboos, they confirmed a false and sentimental reading of her work.

On the other side were Akhmatova's close friends, concerned to reverse the watering-down process. The publication of Lydia Chukovskaya's journals in the 1970s and 1980s in Paris contained genuinely new material and served to counter the endlessly repeated clichés about Akhmatova. Chukovskaya documented her continual, and cultural as well as political, opposition to the Soviet régime. The writings of Emma Gerstein, Joseph Brodsky, Yevgeny Rein and Anatoly Nayman in the 1980s took a similar approach.

Nadezhda Mandelstam's memoirs are a special case. The first volume, *Hope Against Hope* (English edition 1970), contains much authentic detail on the years common to Akhmatova and the author. In reading it, however, I couldn't avoid the feeling that Nadezhda Mandelstam, victim of her own eloquent narrative style, has a tendency to 'literarize' reality. Its sequel, *Hope Abandoned* (English edition 1974), is characterized by a growing ambivalence, not to say love-hate, towards her dead friend. Akhmatova's social milieu is also caustically dismissed. By the end of the book the author herself is the only one in the right, a self-styled equal of the great poet.

This distortion of Akhmatova in Nadezhda Mandelstam's writing is partly attributable to unresolved conflicts between the two, but is also connected with the fact that Osip Mandelstam's rehabilitation was far less successful than Anna Akhmatova's. For a wife and widow whose whole life had been devoted to a husband outlawed, silenced and persecuted to death, this situation must in the long term have been unbearable. The whole meaning of her life was at stake. Had Mandelstam been as honoured after his death as Akhmatova, Nadezhda would have been the widow of a tragic king. But from her point of view she had succeeded merely in becoming a lady-in-waiting, and not the highest-ranking, to a tragic queen. She did not appreciate, however, that although Akhmatova experienced a measure of official acceptance such as Mandelstam never remotely approached, her true poetic status was never clearly and unambiguously acknowledged.

The committee that met in an office of the Central Committee on Moscow's Old Square on 20 October 1988 made Soviet Party and Russian literary history at the same time. All the members and candidates of the Politburo were present, including the reformer Yakovlev and the opponent of reform Ligachev, Foreign Minister Shevardnadze and Defence Minister Yazov. And in order to ensure that the explosive subject was properly handled, Mikhail Gorbachev chaired the meeting in person.

The formal business of the meeting was the processing of two applications. The Union of Soviet Writers and the Leningrad Regional Party Committee had proposed to the country's highest authority that the official attitude to the deceased writers Mikhail Zoshchenko and Anna Akhmatova should at last be publicly revised. In nineteen lines of the minutes of this meeting of the Politburo, classified as 'Top Secret', the Resolution of the Central Committee of the Communist Party of the Soviet Union (then still termed 'All-Union Communist Party/Bolsheviks') of 14 August 1946 was declared invalid.

The Politburo resolved

that the said Resolution distorted Leninist principles of collaboration with the artistic intelligentsia, and that important Soviet writers were exposed to gross and unfounded treatment.

The Party, pursuant to the policy in the field of literature and art which it is conducting under conditions of
revolutionary *perestroika*, has in practice disavowed and
overruled those theses and conclusions, the good name
of the said writers is hereby restored, and their works are
given back to the Soviet reader.
The CC CPSU resolves:
To rescind the Resolution of the CC A[ll-Union]CP(b)
'On the Journals "Zvezda" and "Leningrad"' as errone-
ous.
    Secretary of the CC CPSU   [signed]   *M. Gorbachev*

Without wishing to belittle the achievements of the
father of *perestroika*, some peculiarities of this undoubtedly
well-meaning document must be pointed out. First, it
is not a Resolution in the strict sense of the term, not an
official injunction with the purpose of controlling events
which are imminent or expected in the future. Since
spring 1986, taking it at the very latest, when the weekly
Ogonyok had printed poems by Nikolay Gumilyov and
Pasternak's *Doctor Zhivago* had also been published, an
irreparable breach had been blown in the Soviet literary
taboo-structure. Akhmatova's poems and Zoshchenko's
stories were far from being the most explosive texts
that it suddenly became permissible to print in October
1988.
And it was not only literature and the media that, from
the Party's viewpoint, were out of control at this time.
The Chernobyl disaster, the Armenian earthquake, the
national conflicts in Kazakhstan and the Caucasus,
Matthias Rust's landing in Red Square, as well as less spec-
tacular economic changes, all indicated that the exercise
of power in the giant Soviet empire was sliding towards
catastrophe.
Gorbachev's team was constantly overtaken by events.

Пролетарии всех стран, соединяйтесь!

Коммунистическая Партия Советского Союза. ЦЕНТРАЛЬНЫЙ КОМИТЕТ

СОВЕРШЕННО СЕКРЕТНО

ПРОТОКОЛ № 138

ЗАСЕДАНИЯ ПОЛИТБЮРО ЦЕНТРАЛЬНОГО КОМИТЕТА КПСС

от 20 октября 1988 года

Председательствовал т.Горбачев М.С.

Присутствовали:

Члены Политбюро ЦК т.т.Зайков Л.Н., Лигачев Е.К.,
Медведев В.А., Рыжков Н.И., Слюньков Н.Н.,
Чебриков В.М., Шеварднадзе Э.А., Яковлев А.Н.
Кандидаты в члены Политбюро ЦК т.т.Бирюкова А.П.,
Власов А.В., Лукьянов А.И., Маслюков Ю.Д.,
Разумовский Г.П., Талызин Н.В., Язов Д.Т.
Секретарь ЦК т.Бакланов О.Д.

ХV. <u>О постановлении ЦК ВКП(б) от 14 августа 1946 года</u>
<u>"О журналах "Звезда" и "Ленинград".</u>
(т.т.Горбачев, Зайков, Лигачев, Медведев, Рыжков,
Слюньков, Чебриков, Шеварднадзе, Яковлев)

Рассмотрев обращения в ЦК КПСС Союза писателей СССР
(т.Маркова Г.М.) и Ленинградского обкома КПСС (т.Соловьева Ю.Ф.)
об отмене постановления ЦК ВКП(б) от 14 августа 1946 года
"О журналах "Звезда" и "Ленинград", ЦК КПСС отмечает, что в
указанном постановлении ЦК ВКП(б) были искажены ленинские
принципы работы с художественной интеллигенцией, необоснован-
ной, грубой проработке подвергались видные советские писатели.

Проводимая партией в условиях революционной перестройки
политика в области литературы и искусства практически дезавуиро-
вала и преодолела эти положения и выводы, доброе имя писателей
восстановлено, а их произведения возвращены советскому читателю.

ЦК КПСС постановляет:

Постановление ЦК ВКП(б) "О журналах "Звезда" и "Ленинград"
отменить как ошибочное.

СЕКРЕТАРЬ ЦК КПСС   М.ГОРБАЧЕВ

*'Top secret' minute of the Politburo Meeting of 20 October 1988 rescinding
the August 1946 Resolution of the Central Committee. This document,
bearing the signature of Mikhail Gorbachev, although not mentioning her
name, effectively marks Akhmatova's posthumous rehabilitation*

Politicians seemed to be trying to assuage the public critical appetite and new hunger for truth by feeding it with ever more significant revelations from the past and examples of justice being done in the present. Resolutions such as the above were a part of this process. Little by little, the whole of Soviet history was being called into question. The Party leadership was under pressure of time.

Writers too were in a hurry. When the Politburo met on 20 October 1988, major publications by and on Anna Akhmatova were ready at the printers. The centenary of the poet's birth was approaching. Books and special editions of periodicals had to appear in time for their market. Reconsideration of Stalin's and Zhdanov's twenty-two-year-old injuries was therefore merely a belated reflection of an accomplished fact, little more than a symbolic gesture.

However, since symbolism is a material part of poetry, and especially so in Akhmatova's case, Gorbachev's Resolution should be taken seriously and its content duly assessed. In this respect the text is scant indeed. It is couched in the wooden style that typifies statements by the Russian leadership to this day; and the validity of the reference to 'Leninist principles' looks particularly tarnished when it is recalled that Gumilyov was shot under Lenin's leadership. The fact is that the members of the Politburo were unable to change their spots. In one important point this new Resolution is incorrect even for its time.

In August 1946 the two Leningrad journals had been sharply criticized and their editors and other staff had received severe reprimands. Zoshchenko had been smeared before the whole nation as a 'scoundrel' and Akhmatova as a 'whore'. This 1946 Resolution, with others, had been remembered annually in the press ever since, and the word 'whore', especially, remained fixed in the consciousness of the prudish Russian public, becoming emblematically attached to the poet's name.

Zhdanov's official standing, however, remained unchallenged. Until the late 1980s, the *Great Soviet Encyclopedia* contained under 'Zhdanov' not only the entry on Stalin's chief ideologue but also towns called Zhdanov and Zhdanovsk (named after Akhmatova's arch-enemy in the year of Akhmatova's death), a village of Zhdanovka, a museum and two metallurgical combines with the name. The University of Leningrad also bore the ideologue's name, and, irony of ironies, the last flat in which Akhmatova lived was situated in the Leningrad city district named Zhdanov.

If the test of any attempt at rehabilitation is the extent to which human dignity is restored, we find in the Resolution of 1988 a situation the very reverse of that relating to official treatment of Zhdanov. A Resolution that states that the 'good name' of writers who have been humiliated and slandered is 'restored', and yet does not name those names, simply continues the old humiliations and slanders by other means.

*

> The cunning moon
> Hiding by the gates saw how
> I exchanged my posthumous fame
> For that evening.
> Now they will forget me,
> My books will rot in the cupboard.
> They will call
> No street or stanza Akhmatova.

These lines were written on 27 January 1946, shortly after Isaiah Berlin's second visit to Leningrad. The fear expressed here may be interpreted as Akhmatova's presentiment of the state's revenge. As a result of the night-time visit by the foreigner under suspicion of espionage, she feared that her writings would be banned and that her immortality as a poet would be thwarted for bureaucratic reasons. Earlier, during her war-time stay in Tashkent, she had instinctively foreseen Zhdanov's sentence and expressed her fears in the dramatic fragment entitled 'Enuma elish' (ancient Babylonian meaning 'Up there'), the fragment which she would have liked to give her Guest from the Future as a good-bye present but which she had burnt on her return to Leningrad in 1944, thinking it might get her into trouble.

These lines, however, bear another interpretation. They can be taken as presenting a Faustian bargain: love against immortality. That November evening Isaiah Berlin not only entered the room at 34 Fontanka with the Modigliani drawing on the bare wall which had survived civil war and siege, but he also landed in the middle of *Poem Without a Hero*, the unfinished work that had been its author's true reality ever since 1940. Hence the breathless italic stanza about the Guest on the one hand and the literal fear that as a result of the 'bargain' there will never be an 'Akhmatova stanza', let alone an 'Akhmatova street', in the above-quoted lines on the other: in return for a scrap of joy, the poet will have to pay the highest price, that of poetry itself.

Akhmatova's desire to attain immortality through her own special stanza form has a direct bearing on *Poem*. Many years later she advised the young Brodsky that if he wanted to write a great poem he should find a metrical form that was uniquely his own. Every great poet, she told him, had produced his own prosodic form – Pushkin the celebrated '*Onegin* stanza', Byron his own stanza form, and in *Poem* Akhmatova, too, had invented her own form. The view, widespread in literary circles, that the 'Akhmatova stanza' was not entirely original, but imitative of a metrical scheme of Mikhail Kuzmin, could have hurt her almost more than all the infamous attacks on her by the Party apparat.

In the end, Isaiah Berlin did no harm to the Akhmatova stanza. *Poem* was at last completed in 1962, and he entered literary history as an important male muse. As such, he had arrived at just the right biographical moment to light the fuse of inspiration. Muses are not required to do more; everything else is accomplished by fate and genius.

As far as 'Akhmatova Street' is concerned, another muse appeared, that of history. The city soviet of Odessa obeyed Clio's decree in 1987: Ukraine Street was renamed after Anna Akhmatova. The Party's official distancing from Zhdanov, however, was still a year off. As everybody knows, parties are not visited by muses and are therefore hard to inspire.

In the early 1980s two Russian women shared a concern not over Akhmatova's immortality, about which neither had any doubt, but rather about how her immortality could be demonstrated to the living. Lyudmila Karachkina and Lyudmila Shuravlyova were colleagues at the Crimean Astrophysical Institute at Nauchny. Astronomers have the right to name celestial bodies they have discovered, and in 1982 they decided to name a planet after the poet. This being the Soviet Union, of course they had to submit the name for approval and ratification.

Asteroid No. 3067 was first sighted in Finland in 1938, and another sighting was recorded in 1962 at the Brooklyn Observatory. Both these, however, were single observations with little scientific description. In 1972, 1977 and 1980 the asteroid was seen from Nauchny, although its orbit could not be calculated. In 1982, however, between 14 October and 9 November (the day of Brezhnev's death), the two Russian astronomers obtained five separate observations, from which they were able to ascertain the planet's orbit. Two Japanese specialists, Furuta and Nakano, with a high reputation for the calculation of orbits of astral bodies, were able to update the results of earlier observations.

According to these, the planet is approximately spherical in shape, nine kilometres in diameter, with an average distance from the sun of 336 million kilometres and a minimal distance from the earth of 141 million kilometres. The next opposition was calculated to be due on 1 March 1996, when the planet would be in the constellation of Leo and have a star size of 15, distinctly small.

I have this information from a letter from Lyudmila Karachkina of September 1995, and am not at all sure if I correctly understand all the terminology she uses. One thing, however, I do understand fully. In the last sentence of this letter the word 'star' occurs three times, *zvezda* in Russian, the same word as the title of the Leningrad journal banned by Zhdanov. And so Akhmatova has been given her own *Zvezda*, and justice has been done, if not on earth, then in heaven at least.

Lyudmila Karachkina told me of one astonishing coincidence. She had studied at Rostov State University, where the Rector had been a great lover of poetry and astronomy. His name was Yury Andreyevich Zhdanov, and he was a son of the ideologue. As a young man he had spent several years in an unhappy dynastic marriage to Stalin's daughter Svetlana before retiring from Kremlin life. The chair of astronomy at Rostov University was his creation.

Lyudmila Karachkina wrote in reserved terms about the obtaining of approval for the name of her planet: 'People never like remembering the bad things; we often had no idea whether the name would ever get through or not, and so we'd use formulae like "Soviet poetess", in keeping with the time.' But at last an 'institute of theoretical astronomy responsible for the co-ordination of research on astral bodies in the Soviet Union' issued a certificate in the name of the Soviet Academy of Sciences announcing that Asteroid No. 3067 was named 'Akhmatova' – six years after its orbit and salient characteristics had been established. The certificate, signed on 7 July 1988 – it must therefore have contributed to the pressure on the Politburo to rescind the Zhdanov Resolution on 20 October of that year – bore the following rubric, in English, explaining its name:

Named in honor of Anna Andreevna Akhmatova (1889–1966), outstanding poetess, awarded an honorary doctorate by the University of Oxford.

In the 1980s the observatory at Nauchny became a kind of rehabilitation centre for Russian poets and artists who at various times had been banned, incarcerated, killed, driven to suicide or silenced. The list of names of astral bodies discovered by Karachkina and Shuravlyova reads like an astronomically precise revisionist chart of Soviet cultural policy. Here are some of the entries:

No.	Year	Name
5759	1980	Mikhail Zoshchenko
3508	1980	Boris Pasternak
3067	1982	Anna Akhmatova
3345	1982	Andrey Tarkovsky
3469	1982	Mikhail Bulgakov
3511	1982	Marina Tsvetayeva
4556	1987	Nikolay Gumilyov
5808	1987	Isaak Babel

*

Although the name of Osip Mandelstam is a striking gap in this list, I nurture the hope of another addition. To uplift the spirits of all humiliated and disgraced writers I should like to see an asteroid bearing the proud and at the same time modest name 'Guest from the Future'.

Appendix

Résumé from the head of the Leningrad Branch of the Ministry of State Security to Andrey Zhdanov, 15 August 1946

This document is the only one to be found in the relevant archives of the Russian Federation that is entirely concerned with Anna Akhmatova. It is clear from its date that between the Central Committee Resolution of 14 August and the meeting of the Leningrad branch of the Union of Soviet Writers at the Smolny Institute, Leningrad, on 16 August 1946, the Party ideologue Andrey Zhdanov was busy preparing his speech for the latter occasion. He urgently ordered a bundle of compromising material (*kompromat* in Soviet jargon) on the two 'chief accused', Anna Akhmatova and Mikhail Zoshchenko, from the relevant quarters, including an official résumé of what was known about each by the MGB. While the coverage of the résumé on Zoshchenko is almost complete (see D.L. Babichenko (ed.), pp. 215–26), that on Akhmatova is extremely sketchy.

The following translation preserves the abbreviated and unpolished style in which the résumé is written. The document contains a number of errors of fact as well as statements that Berlin and Akhmatova would never have said in the words alleged – for example, Isaiah Berlin's 'statement' on first meeting Akhmatova. And the MGB's informers are inaccurate on certain biographical details; they have Akhmatova's year of birth wrong and, in the invariable manner of the secret police from the Cheka onwards, are unable to clear their minds completely of Lev Gumilyov's executed father's initials. However, editorial correction seems uncalled for, since it is not this or that particular error of fact that is significant in this document, which is a linguistic monument built of untruth.

Résumé: From Dir MGB L Dpt Rodionov re Akhmatova /SU/
15.8.46/23–30/

Akhmatova A.A., b. 1892, of nobility, began lit. act-y 1910, having won pop. as foremost represent. of Acmeism, one of whose founders was her f. husband, the poet N. Gumilyov

In 24–26 lit. output fell sharply, published almost nothing. Only in 40 was 'From Six Books' published. In VOV [Great Patriotic War, i.e. Second World War] poems by A. publ. in 'Zvezda', 'Leningrad', 'Leningradsk. Almanakh' etc.

Gumilyov separated from A. in 17, arrested and exec. in 21 for active partic. in SR [Socialist Revolutionary, anti-Bolshevik] rising.

Second husband *Shileyko V.K.*, Assyriologist, tutor to children of Count Sheremetyev, a man with religious-myst. interests. A. lived with him for a short time separated and married *N.N. Punin*, a prof. at the All-Russ Academy of Arts, with whom she lived 16 years. In 36 Punin left and married another woman, but A. went on living in his flat. A. intended *Garshin V.G.* to be her next husband – a pathologist and anatomical specialist, deputy director of VIEM [All-Union Institute of Experimental Medicine]. During A.'s evacuation in Tashkent Garshin obtained permission for her return to L., however on her return G. suddenly told her he could no longer live with her.

At pres. A. lives with her son Gumilyov L.N. (age 30, post-graduate student at LGU [Leningrad State University]) In 38 NIG received a sentence for belonging to an antisov youth org-ion, but was rel. in 45 to join the RKKA [Workers' and Peasants' Red Army] and took part in action on Germ.-held terr.

A. is const. in reduced mat. circumstances, and lives in a poorly furnished flat, in need of clothing and footwear and short of food because apparently her rations are used by the Punin family. However A. takes no steps to better her mat. circs, leads a humble shut-off life, avoids partic. in SSP [Union of Soviet Writers] events and is reluctant to make public app-ces.

In the West A. enjoys a very high standing and enormous popularity. Among the cultured intelligentsia she wears the halo of a poetess who is unacknowledged in the Soviet Union. Abroad she is compared with Sappho, and Chukovsky has called her 'Pushkin's great successor'. According to information received by the Directorate, in 45–46 a cycle of poems by A. was broadcast in Britain, articles in praise of her poetry were published, and an edition of her poems in English translation was in preparation.

Describing her last trip to Moscow in May 46, A. said: 'All the for. embassies were represented in the Hall of Columns, the British prominent among them. The introducer said that A. was the first poetess in the world. I was bombarded with telephone calls from for. corr-s asking me for interviews, autographs, just wanting to set eyes on me.'

During the war A. is known to have received food parcels from a European or European-Amer. aid association. The interest shown in A. by a First Secretary at the British Embassy in Moscow, BERLIN, a doctor of philosophy and connoisseur of Russian literature, merits special attention. When Berlin visited L. in Nov 45 V.N. Orlov took him to see A. On being introduced to her, B. said: 'I have come to L. specially to pay tribute to you, the foremost and the latest of European poets, not only in my name but also in that of the whole tradition of British culture. In Oxford you are considered a legend of the highest order. In Britain your work is translated with the reverence accorded to Sappho . . .' On the foll. day B. again visited A., and in their conversation lasting from 22 to 07 hrs next morning they discussed ?? lit. and phil. subjects. B. promised to send A. all editions of her poetry in English, 'he spoke openly of the desirability of using unoff. channels for this purpose, and asked A. about practical ways of maintaining illegal forms of contact with her.'

Their third meeting, in the course of which they discussed emigration of Whites (we have no substantive details on this conversation), ended at 4 o'clock in the morning.

After B. had left Russia, A., afraid, as she put it, that 'evil tongues' might twist the facts, said: 'It was the initiative of others that made B. seek a meeting with me. It is clear that someone "high up" in Britain or in the British Embassy ordered an investigation of how I live, with a view to some kind of speculation about my name and reputation, as a poet and as a woman.'

*

On 18.8.44 A. said to one of her friends: 'I've virtually stopped publishing my poetry, because Russian poetry seems fated to be in an illeg. position at the present time . . . I am not prepared to give my poems to publishers now because there's no guarantee that something suspicious won't be found in some innocent line and lead to my poems being banned.' To another male friend in Apr. 46 A. said: 'There's something illegal about me . . . My "Poem Without a Hero" has been banned on the pretext that it is impossible to understand. Surely it can't be the case that our country cannot afford to have a single poet who is understand-able to everyone who understands poetry.'

'Poem Without a Hero', which has not been passed for publication, is circulating illegally in manuscript among the liter-ary intellectuals and staff of the univ-ies of M., L. and Tashkent at the present time

In a conversation with a student named Ioffe (aged 21) of Herzen University, an admirer of A., she said: '. . . I am a believer. And therefore I do not believe in death. For non-believers that is a paradox: for me it is a necessary conclusion'

Among A.'s closest contacts in L. are O. Berggolts, her husband Makogonenko, the poet Spassky, and A.N. Orlov, a professor at the Inst. of literature

Chronologies

ANNA ANDREYEVNA AKHMATOVA (Gorenko)

1889   Born on 23 (11 according to the Julian calendar) June at Bolshoy Fontan on the Black Sea coast near Odessa, then part of Russia and now in the Ukraine. The third of five children. Her father was a naval engineer who took a post in the civil service in 1890, in which year the family moved to Pavlovsk before settling in Tsarskoye Selo nearer St Petersburg.

1907   Enrols in the Faculty of Law at the Kiev College for Women.

1910   Marriage to the poet Nikolay Stepanovich Gumilyov; honeymoon in Paris; the couple settle in Tsarskoye Selo.

1911   Gumilyovs visit Paris again, where A. meets Modigliani. Return to Tsarskoye Selo.
       With four other poets including Osip Mandelstam, the Acmeist group formed.

1912   March: First book of poems, *Evening*, published in a small edition.
       October: Son Lev born.

1914   Second book of poems, *Rosary*, wins its author great currency.
       August: Gumilyov volunteers for the front.

1917   A. and Gumilyov separate.
       Third book of poems, *White Flock*.

1918   A. and Gumilyov divorce.
       Autumn: Marriage to the Assyriologist Vladimir

Shileyko. The couple take a room in Fountain House on the Fontanka Canal.

1920   Works as a librarian at the Institute of Agronomy.

1921   Leaves Shileyko.
        August: Gumilyov shot without trial for alleged anti-Bolshevik conspiracy.
        Fourth book of poems, *Plantain*.

1922   Fifth book of poems, *Anno Domini MCMXXI*.

1925   A substantial selection of A.'s poems appear in an anthology of twentieth-century Russian poetry, the last of her poems to be published in the Soviet Union until 1940.

1926   Moves in with the Punin family in Fountain House. Begins studies of Pushkin.

1920s–mid-1930s   Writes few poems. Son Lev is brought up largely by Gumilyov's parents.

1928   A. and Shileyko divorce.

1935   Punin and Lev Gumilyov arrested, then released.

1935–40   Writes *Requiem*.

1937   Separation from Punin.

1938   March: Lev Gumilyov rearrested and held.

1939   July: Lev Gumilyov released for military service.

1940   Meets Marina Tsvetayeva, returned to the Soviet Union from Paris.
        Effective ban on A.'s work briefly lifted.
        Summer: *From Six Books*, containing poems from previously published books and new poems.
        Autumn: *From Six Books* withdrawn from bookshops and libraries.
        October: First heart attack.
        Begins *Poem Without a Hero*, which she does not acknowledge as finished until 1962.

1941   September: Speaks on radio during the Siege of Leningrad.

1942   Evacuated from Leningrad to Moscow by order of the Central Committee of the Communist Party of Leningrad. Moves to Tashkent.

1943   *Selected Poems* published in Tashkent, heavily censored.

1944   May: Returns to Moscow, where reads to an enthusiastic audience.
        June: Returns to Leningrad.

1945   Returns to the Fontanka to live with the Punins. Lev Gumilyov, who has fought in the war, rejoins the household.
        November: Isaiah Berlin's visit to A. in Fountain House on the Fontanka.

1946   January: Isaiah Berlin's brief good-bye visit, after which A.'s room is bugged.
        Selected Poems in preparation in Moscow, heavily censored.
        Poems 1909–1945 in preparation in Moscow/Leningrad, then almost completely destroyed.
        April: Triumphal readings in Moscow.
        August: Resolution of the Central Committee of the Soviet Communist Party *On the Journals 'Zvezda' and 'Leningrad'*, attacking the two journals for publishing A. and Zoshchenko.
        September: Stalin's cultural watchdog, Andrey Zhdanov, makes a speech to the Leningrad branch of the Union of Soviet Writers initiating the Party's smear campaign against A. and Zoshchenko and laying down an anti-Western line to be followed by Soviet writers and artists. A. and Zoshchenko are immediately expelled from the Union of Soviet Writers and publication of their works is banned.
        September: Punin arrested.

1949   November: Lev Gumilyov rearrested and receives an extended prison camp sentence.

1950   Publishes a cycle of propagandistic poems 'In Praise of Peace' in the hope that it will help towards Lev's release.

1952   Forced move from Fountain House. Moves with the Punins to Krasnaya Konnitsa.

1953   Death of Punin in a Siberian camp.

1954   May: British delegation of students visits Leningrad and meets A. and Zoshchenko; A. again incurs disfavour with the Party for displeasing the delegation by refusing to give a full answer to a leading question.

1955   A. granted a small dacha in the village of Komarovo near Leningrad.

1956   May/June: Lev Gumilyov released from camp and exonerated by Supreme Soviet in the general thaw following Khrushchev's denunciation of Stalin in February. 'Non-Meeting' with Isaiah Berlin, visiting Russia in August.

1958   *Poems*, edited (and severely censored) by Aleksey Surkov; the volume contains many translations from Far Eastern languages.
New poems published in Soviet periodicals.

1961   *Poems 1909–1960*; this volume is also censored.

Early 1960s   Editions of A.'s poems published (without her authorization) in the West (France, Italy, Germany, etc).

1963   Publication of *Requiem* in Munich 'without the author's knowledge or consent'.

1964   Trip to Catania to receive the Etna-Taormina Prize.

1965   Trip (by rail) to Britain to receive an honorary doctorate from the University of Oxford. Sees Isaiah Berlin again. Visits old friends in Paris on return journey.
The Flight of Time, less heavily censored than previous books of verse.

November: Suffers another heart attack, in Moscow, spending three months in hospital.

1966   Dies on 5 March, in a sanatorium near Moscow.

1976   *Poem Without a Hero* published in the Soviet Union, with a few stanzas excluded.

1987   The full text of *Requiem* published in the Soviet Union.

1988   May: The Soviet Academy of Sciences officially names Asteroid No. 3067 'Akhmatova'.
        October: The Politburo rescinds the August 1946 Resolution of the Soviet CP's Central Committee *On the Journals 'Zvezda' and 'Leningrad'*, an indirect rehabilitation of A.

ISAIAH BERLIN

1909   Born on 6 June in Riga, then part of the Russian Empire, today capital of Latvia, of Russian-speaking parents. Father the owner of a timber business.

1917–20   Berlin family live in Petrograd.

1920   Berlins return briefly to Riga.

1921   Berlin family emigrate to Britain, living first in Surbiton, then in Kensington, London.

1920s   Attends St Paul's School.

1928–32   Scholar at Corpus Christi College, Oxford. Reads Greats and PPE (Firsts).

1932–8   Lecturer in Philosophy, University of Oxford, and Fellow of All Souls College.

1938   Becomes a Fellow and Tutor in Philosophy at New College.

1939   *Karl Marx: His Life and Environment*.

1941   In New York for the Ministry of Information.

1942–6   Serves at the Foreign Office as First Secretary: in the British Embassy in Washington, reporting on the changing political mood in the United States, and for several months in 1945 in the British Embassy in Moscow. A selection of despatches to Whitehall from Washington drafted by him published (1981) as *Washington Despatches 1941–1945*.

1945   November: Meeting with Anna Akhmatova at her flat in Fountain House on the Fontanka Canal. During this spell in Russia, also meets and befriends Boris Pasternak.

1950   Having decided to give up philosophy for the history of ideas, returns as a Fellow to All Souls.

1953   *The Hedgehog and the Fox: An Essay on Tolstoy's View of History*.

1954   *Historical Inevitability*.

1956   Marries Aline Halban, daughter of the eminent European banker Pierre de Gunzbourg.

1957   Elected to the Chichele Chair of Social and Political Theory at the University of Oxford; his inaugural lecture, 'Two Concepts of Liberty', comes to be accepted as a classic account of the subject (later included in *Four Essays on Liberty*, 1969). Knighted the same year.

1966–75   First President of Wolfson College, Oxford.

1971   Appointed to the Order of Merit.

1974–8   President of the British Academy.

1978   *Russian Thinkers*: *Concepts and Categories*.

1979   *Against the Current*.

1980   *Personal Impressions*.

1990   *The Crooked Timber of Humanity*.

1993   *The Magus of the North.*

1996   *The Sense of Reality.*

1997   *The Proper Study of Mankind.*
       Dies on 5 November, in Oxford.

Glossary of Names

ALEKSANDROV, GEORGY (1908–61): Philosopher and Party functionary, one of the organizers of the campaign against the journals *Zvezda* and *Leningrad*.

ALIGER, MARGARITA (1915–92): Poet, friend of A. from 1941. Organized A.'s broadcasts on Leningrad radio during the Siege.

ANREP, BORIS (1883–1969): Poet and mosaic artist who held a special place in A.'s affections in the years before 1917. A. dedicated more than thirty poems to him. Emigrated to Britain in 1917. A. met him again in Paris in 1965.

ARDOVA (OLSHEVSKAYA), NINA (1908–91): Actress, a close friend of A. from the early 1940s. A. stayed with her on her Moscow visits.

BERGGOLTS, OLGA (1910–75): Leningrad poet and prose-writer, a friend of A. from 1928; frequently demanded the annulment of Zhdanov's Resolution condemning A. and Zoshchenko.

BERIA, LAVRENTY (1889–1953): Head of the Soviet secret police from 1938; executed after Stalin's death.

BLOK, ALEKSANDR (1880–1921): Father of Russian Symbolism, and of Russian twentieth-century poetry. Acquainted with A. from 1911. Each dedicated several poems to the other.

BOWRA, SIR MAURICE (1898–1971): From 1922 a Fellow and 1938–70 Warden of Wadham College, Oxford. Legendary scholar, critic and wit. Edited two books of Russian verse in translation (1943, 1948) which included poems by A.

BREZHNEV, LEONID (1906–82): Chairman of the Presidium of the Supreme Soviet 1960–4 and from 1966 General Secretary of the

CPSU. Jointly authorized A.'s trip to Italy to receive the Etna-Taormina Prize in 1964.

BRODSKY, JOSEPH (1940–96): Poet and critic of leading stature from the 1970s. Sentenced to five years' hard labour for 'social parasitism' (commuted). Hounded into exile in the United States in 1972. Awarded the Nobel Prize for Literature in 1987. One of A.'s closest friends in her last years.

CHUKOVSKAYA, LYDIA (1907–96): Novelist and publisher's editor. First met A. in 1938 and became one of her closest friends and confidantes. Worked on *From Six Books* (published briefly in 1940) with A. while an editor at Goslitizdat. Her journals recording her conversations with A., covering the years 1938–41 and 1952–66, are one of the most important sources on A.'s life and work. Daughter of Korney Chukovsky.

CHUKOVSKY, KORNEY (1882–1969): Poet, translator and essayist. Acquainted with A. from 1912, but came to know her better only in the last years of her life, when he wrote an appreciative essay on her work. Awarded an honorary doctorate by the University of Oxford in 1962. Father of Lydia Chukovskaya.

CZAPSKI, JOZEF (1896–1993): Writer and information officer in General Anders's Polish Army in Exile; met A. during her wartime stay in Tashkent. She dedicated a poem to him.

EHRENBURG, ILYA (1891–1967): Novelist and journalist; author of memoirs *People, Years and Life* (mid-1960s). First met A. in Paris in 1910. Made representations on A.'s behalf several times in the 1950s.

EIKHENBAUM, BORIS (1886–1959): Leading literary historian and Formalist critic; author of an early book on A. (1922) from which Zhdanov twisted the phrase 'nun and whore' into his infamous slogan against A.

FADEYEV, ALEKSANDR (1901–56): Novelist (*The Young Guard*, 1945, etc), Secretary-General of the Union of Soviet Writers 1946–53. Although a participant in the campaign against A., he sought informally to mitigate its consequences for her. Committed suicide after Khrushchev's denunciation of Stalin at the 20th Party Congress.

GARSHIN, VLADIMIR (1887–1956): Leningrad doctor who proposed marriage to A. during the Second World War but changed his mind when she returned to Russia from Tashkent.

GERSTEIN, EMMA (b. 1903): Literary scholar who first met A. in 1934 and became one of her closest friends, helping her in efforts to obtain her son Lev's release from prison and prison camp. In the 1980s she began to publish her memoirs of A.

GORBACHEV, MIKHAIL (b. 1931): General Secretary of the CPSU 1985–91, President of the Supreme Soviet 1988–91, head of state 1989–91. His liberal reforms (*perestroika* and *glasnost*), contrary to his intentions, led to the break-up of the Soviet Union. In 1988 he signed a document on behalf of the Central Committee rescinding the August 1946 Resolution against A. and Zoshchenko.

GORENKO, VIKTOR (1896–1976): Emigré brother of A., who was in correspondence with her in the 1960s.

GUMILYOV, NIKOLAY (1886–1921): Poet and founder of the Acmeist group of poets in St Petersburg in 1912. Married to A. 1910–18. Shot by the Cheka in 1921 for alleged 'participation' in Professor Tagantsev's 'conspiracy'.

GUMILYOV, LEV (1912–92): Son of A. and Nikolay Gumilyov. Arrested then released in 1935; rearrested in 1938 and held in Leningrad for seventeen months, then released to serve in the army (took part in the liberation of Berlin); arrested again in 1949 after which he spent seven years in a labour camp before being amnestied in 1956. Became a professor of oriental ethnography at Leningrad University.

HAIGHT, AMANDA (1939–89): American literary historian, author of the first English-language biography of A. (1976). A friend of A. for the last three years of her life and accompanied her to Oxford for the award of her honorary doctorate in 1965.

KAMINSKAYA, ANNA (b. 1939): Daughter of Irina Punina; accompanied A. to Oxford for the award of her honorary doctorate in 1965. Art historian.

KHRUSHCHEV, NIKITA (1894–1971): First Secretary of the Central Committee of the CPSU 1953–64. His denunciation of Stalin at the 20th Party Congress in February 1956 triggered off mass releases and rehabilitations, e.g. for Lev Gumilyov.

KOPELEV, LEV (b. 1912): Literary historian and translator. In the gulag 1945–55; emigrated to Germany in 1980. A friend of A. from 1962, he has written memoirs of her.

LEBEDEV, VLADIMIR (1915–66): Khrushchev's private secretary. He put the case for publication of Solzhenitsyn's *One Day in the Life of Ivan Denisovich* (1962) and wanted complete literary rehabilitation for A.

MANDELSTAM, OSIP (1891–1938): First acquainted with A. as a fellow member of the Acmeist group of poets in 1914; a closer friendship developed in the late 1920s. When M. was exiled to Voronezh as a result of his satirical poem on Stalin, A. visited him there. She dedicated a number of poems to him and wrote memoirs of him.

MANDELSTAM, NADEZHDA (1899–1980): Wife of Osip Mandelstam; teacher. A close friend of A. from 1924; she gives A. an important place in her memoirs (English editions 1970 and 1974).

MIKOYAN, ANASTAS (1895–1978): As a member of the Politburo and a supporter of Khrushchev, chaired a special committee in 1956 that authorized immediate releases from the gulag; Lev Gumilyov owed his release in that year to this committee.

MODIGLIANI, AMEDEO (1884–1920): Met A. in Paris in 1910 and made sixteen portrait drawings of her.

NAYMAN, ANATOLY (b. 1936): Poet and translator, A.'s literary and personal secretary from 1962. Author of a memoir on A. (1991).

ORLOVA (KOPELEVA), RAISA (1918–89): Wife of Lev Kopelev. Met A. in 1962. She gave a long interview with her husband which includes much detail about A.'s last years.

PASTERNAK, BORIS (1890–1960): First met A. in 1922 (the year of publication of his first major book of verse *My Sister Life*), and became a close friend. Each dedicated a number of poems to the other.

PROKOFIEV, ALEKSANDR (1900–71): Poet and cultural functionary. Although he participated in the 1946 anti-A. campaign, he tried to put the case against it to Stalin.

PUNIN, NIKOLAY (1888–1953): Art historian. Lived with A. 1924–37; A. continued to live in his flat after their relationship had ended. Arrested in 1935 then released; arrested again in 1949; died in a prison camp in Siberia in 1953.

PUNINA, IRINA (b. 1921): Daughter of Nikolay Punin by his first marriage. After A.'s own separation from Punin, and again after Punin's death, A. lived in her flat. Accompanied A. to Italy to receive the Etna-Taormina Prize in December 1964.

SHILEYKO, VLADIMIR (1891–1930): Assyriologist; A.'s second husband, 1918–21.

SOLZHENITSYN, ALEKSANDR (b. 1918): Met A. in 1962; she read him *Requiem*.

STALIN, JOSEF (1879–1953): Appointed Secretary-General of the Central Committee of the Soviet Communist Party in 1922. When Nikolay Punin and Lev Gumilyov were arrested by the NKVD in 1935, they were released when A. wrote a personal letter to Stalin. Played a decisive part in the campaign against A. and Zoshchenko in August 1946.

SURKOV, ALEKSEY (1899–1983): Poet and cultural functionary; Secretary of the Union of Soviet Writers 1954–9. Pressed for A.'s rehabilitation, and helped her over her visits to Italy and Britain in 1964 and 1965, but in editing her last books of verse he exercised heavy censorship.

TRIPP, BRENDA: British Council official posted in the Soviet Union during the post-war period; subsequently head of the East European Section of the British Council. She played a part in preparations for A.'s visit to Oxford in 1965.

TSVETAYEVA, MARINA (1892–1941): A. met the other doyenne of twentieth-century Russian poetry in Moscow in 1940, twice only, between the latter's return to Russia after years of exile abroad and her suicide the following year in the Tatar town of Yelabuga.

TVARDOVSKY, ALEKSANDR (1910–71): Poet, and as chief editor of the journal *Novy Mir* 1958–70 was at the cutting edge of Soviet literature during that period. Published a number of A.'s poems and an essay on her work.

VIGORELLI, GIANCARLO (b. 1912): Founder-director of the European Community of Writers, which awarded the 1964 Etna-Taormina Prize to A. First met A. in Leningrad in 1963.

YEGOLIN, ALEKSANDR (1896–1959): Literary historian and Party functionary, one of those who prepared A.'s excommunication in August 1946.

ZHDANOV, ANDREY (1896–1948): As Secretary of the Central Committee of the CPSU and in charge of ideological affairs, introduced strict political control, nationalism and anti-Westernism into the arts. In 1940 he had A.'s *From Six Books* withdrawn. In 1946 he implemented the campaign against A. and Zoshchenko.

ZOSHCHENKO, MIKHAIL (1895–1958): Satirical short story writer; one of the most popular of Soviet authors. He and A. knew each other from the 1920s. Their simultaneous expulsion from the Writers' Union in 1946 brought them together. On Z.'s death, A. dedicated a poem to him that she later included in the cycle *A Wreath for the Dead* (no. IX).

Select Bibliography

ANNA AKHMATOVA

Verse

The Complete Poems of Anna Akhmatova, bilingual edition, translated by Judith Hemschemeyer; edited and with an Introduction by Roberta Reeder (including excerpts from *Personal Impressions* by Isaiah Berlin and *Remembering Anna Akhmatova* by Anatoly Nayman); 2 vols, Zephyr Press, Somerville, MA, 1990; revised and enlarged one-volume edition without the Russian texts, Zephyr and Canongate Books, Edinburgh, 1998 (paperback)

Selected Poems, translated by Richard McKane, Bloodaxe Books, 1989 (paperback)

Selected Poems, bilingual edition, translated and introduced by Stanley Kunitz with Max Hayward, Little, Brown, Boston and Toronto, 1973; Collins Harvill, London, 1989 (paperback)

Biographies

Amanda Haight, *Anna Akhmatova: A Poetic Pilgrimage*, Oxford University Press, London and New York, 1976 (paperback, 1990)

Roberta Reeder, *Anna Akhmatova: Poet and Prophet*, St Martin's Press, New York, 1994 and Allison & Busby, London, 1995

Memoirs and criticism

Joseph Brodsky, *Less Than One: Selected Essays* (essay: 'The Keening Muse'), Farrar, Straus & Giroux, New York, 1986; Penguin Books, Harmondsworth, 1987

Lydia Chukovskaya, *The Akhmatova Journals*, Vol. 1: *1938–41*, translated from the author's revised text by Milena Michalski and Sylva Rubashova, poetry translated by Peter Norman; Harvill (HarperCollins), London, 1994

Nadezhda Mandelstam, *Hope Against Hope: A Memoir*, translated by Max Hayward, with an introduction by Clarence Brown; Atheneum Publishers, New York, 1970 and Collins & Harvill Press, London, 1971; Collins Harvill, London, 1989 (paperback)

—— *Hope Abandoned*, Atheneum Publishers, New York, 1972 and Collins & Harvill Press, London, 1974; Collins Harvill, London, 1989 (paperback)

Anatoly Nayman, *Remembering Anna Akhmatova*, edited and translated by Wendy Rosslyn, Introduction by Joseph Brodsky; Henry Holt, New York and Peter Halban, London, 1991

David N. Wells, *Anna Akhmatova: Her Poetry*, Berg, Oxford and Washington, D.C., 1996

ISAIAH BERLIN

Four Essays on Liberty, Oxford University Press, London, 1969

Personal Impressions, Hogarth Press, London, 1980; 2nd (enlarged) edition, Pimlico (Random House), London, 1998 (paperback)

Russian Thinkers, Hogarth Press, London, 1978; Penguin Books, Harmondsworth, 1979 (paperback)

Sources

UNPUBLISHED

Berlin, Isaiah, letters written from British Embassies in Washington and Moscow, 1945, and subsequently from Oxford
—— letters written to, at various times
—— 'Notes on a Visit to Leningrad', November 1945, Public Record Office FO 371/56724
—— 'A Note on Literature and the Arts in the Russian Soviet Federated Socialist Republic in the Closing Months of 1945', Public Record Office FO 371/56725
—— recorded conversation with author, London, August 1995
Rossiysky Tsentr khraneniya sovremennoy dokumentatsii 1954–1989 [Russian Centre for the Conservation of Contemporary Documents 1954–1989 (archives of the Soviet Communist Party)], Moscow
Shukman, Harry, recorded conversation with author, Randolph Hotel, Oxford, 13 August 1995

PUBLISHED

Akhmatova, Anna, *Selected Poems*, translated by Richard McKane, Bloodaxe Books, Newcastle upon Tyne, 1989
—— *The Complete Poems of Anna Akhmatova*, translated by Judith Hemschemeyer; edited and with an Introduction by Roberta Reeder [bilingual edition], Zephyr Press, Somerville, MA, 2 vols, 1990
Babichenko, D.L. (ed.), *'Literaturny front': Istoriya politicheskoy*

tsenzury 1932–1946: Sbornik dokumentov ['The literary front':
    a history of political censorship 1932–1946: a collection of
    documents], Izd. Entsiklopediya rossiyskikh dereven',
    Moscow, 1994

Berlin, Isaiah, *Personal Impressions*, 2nd edition, Pimlico, London,
    1998

Bongard, Willi, *Die Zeit*, Hamburg, 5 February 1963

Chukovskaya, Lidiya, 'Zapiski ob Anne Akhmatovoy' [The
    Akhmatova Journals], II: '1952–62', *Neva* 8/1993

—— *Zapiski ob Anne Akhmatovoy*, II: *1952–1962*, Soglasiye,
    Moscow, 1997

——*Zapiski ob Anne Akhmatovoy*, III: *1963–1966*, Soglasiye,
    Moscow, 1997

Chukovsky, Korney, *Dnevnik 1930–1969* [Diary 1930–1969],
    Sovremennyy Pisatel', Moscow, 1994

'Doklad A. Zhdanova na sobranii partiynogo aktiva i na sobranii
    pisateley v Leningrade' [Speech by A. Zhdanov at a meeting
    of Party activists and at a meeting of writers in Leningrad],
    Pravda, no. 225, 21 September 1946

Gerstein, Emma, 'Iz vospominaniy' [From reminiscences],
    Voprosy Literatury 6/1989

—— 'Anna Akhmatova i Lev Gumilyov: razmyshleniya svide-
    telya' [Anna Akhmatova and Lev Gumilyov: an eye-
    witness's reflections], *Znamya* 9/1995

—— 'Lev Gumilyov – Emme Gerstein. Pis'ma iz lagerya
    (1954–1956)' [Lev Gumilyov to Emma Gerstein. Letters
    from a prison camp (1954–1956)], *Znamya* 9/1995

Gosbezopasnost' i literatura. Na opyte Rossii i Germanii [State secur-
    ity and literature. On the experience of Russia and
    Germany], Rudomino: Fond Genrikha Bellya, 1994

Gumilyov, Lev, 'Inache poeta net' [Otherwise there is no poet]
    (interview), *Literaturnoye Obozreniye* 5/1989

Haight, Amanda, *Anna Akhmatova: A Poetic Pilgrimage*, Oxford
    University Press, 1976

Ivanov, Vyacheslav V., 'Vstrechi s Akhmatovoy' [Encounters
    with Akhmatova], *Znamya* 7/1989

Kuzmina, Yelena, *Anna Akhmatova: Ein Leben im Unbehausten*

[Anna Akhmatova: a homeless life], translated from Russian by Svetlana Geier, Rowohlt, Berlin, 1993

Lakshin, Vladimir, *'Novy mir' vo vremena Khrushcheva. Dnevnik i poputnoye (1953–1964)* [*Novy Mir* under Khrushchev. Diary of an era (1953–1964)], Knizhnaya Palata, Moscow, 1991

Mandelstam, Nadezhda, *Vtoraya kniga* [The second book], Moskovsky Rabochiy, Moscow, 1990

Nayman, Anatoly, 'Rasskazy ob Anne Akhmatovoy' [Stories of Anna Akhmatova], *Novy Mir* 2/1989

—— *Rasskazy ob Anne Akhmatovoy*, Khudozhestvennaya Literatura, Moscow, 1989

Orlova, Raisa and Lev Kopelev, 'Anna vseya Rusi' [Anna of all Russia'], *Literaturnoye Obozreniye* 5/1989

Richter, Hans Werner, *Euterpe von den Ufern der Newa: oder die Ehrung Anna Akhmatowas in Taormina* [Euterpe from the banks of the Neva: or Anna Akhmatova's award in Taormina], Friedenauer Presse, Berlin, 1965 [report for Freies Berlin and Norddeutscher Rundfunk broadcast on 30 January 1965, in book form]

Vilenkin, Vitaly Ya. (ed.), *Vospominaniya ob Anne Akhmatovoy* [Memories of Anna Akhmatova], Sovetsky Pisatel', Moscow, 1991

Zhdanov, Andrey, Speech on Music and Art, 10 February 1948

Zoshchenko, Mikhail, in 'Publikatsiya Yu. Tomashevskogo: M.M. Zoshchenko – Pis'ma, vystupleniya, dokumenty 1943–1958' [M.M. Zoshchenko – letters, speeches and documents 1943–1958: edited by Yu. Tomashevsky], *Druzhba narodov* 3/1988

1   THE MEETING

p. 16: 'I have like all the Three Sisters . . .' IB, Washington to Sir Ponsonby Moore Crosthwaite, British Embassy, Moscow, 12 May 1945.

'I am fascinated . . .' IB, Moscow to his parents, 19 September 1945.

'I go to the theatre . . .' IB, Moscow to his mother, 11 October 1945.

p. 17: 'I had heard that books . . .' IB, 1998, p. 231.

p. 18: 'Mandelstam is . . .' Maurice Bowra, Wadham College to IB, 7 October 1945.

'Akhmatova lives in Leningrad . . .' IB, Washington to Bowra, 7 June 1945.

'the object . . . book of poems'. IB, 1998, p. 232.

pp. 18–19: 'You mean Zoshchenko and Akhmatova? . . .' Ibid., pp. 232–3.

p. 19: 'turned left, crossed . . .', 'We climbed up . . .' Ibid., p. 233.

p. 25: 'Then without any transition . . .', 'In Moscow she told . . .' Vilenkin, p. 243.

pp. 25–6: 'We talked far into the night . . .' Ibid., p. 342.

p. 26: 'We knew that Garshin . . .' Ibid., p. 343.

p. 27: 'Tell me how your health is . . .' Ibid., p. 262.

'Garshin is mentally very ill . . .' Ibid., p. 261.

p. 28: 'Akhmatova has many acquaintances . . .' *Gosbezopasnost' i literatura*, p. 76.

p. 29: 'an idiotic kindergarten . . .' Ibid.

'It was very barely furnished . . .' IB, 1998, p. 233.

p. 30: 'The problem of food . . .' IB, 'Notes on a Visit to Leningrad', § 16, p. 6.

'The room in which . . .' Quoted from Chukovskaya, II, 1997, p. 429.

p. 31: 'Not a word . . .', 'In the stairwell . . .' Ibid., pp. 747, 17.

p. 32: 'These young men . . .' Nayman, Moscow, 1989, p. 162.

'A stately, grey-haired lady . . .' IB, 1998, p. 233.

p.33: 'English universities . . .' Ibid., p. 235.

pp. 33–4: 'we talked about the composer . . .' Ibid.

p. 34: 'She spoke . . . of her first husband . . .' Ibid., pp. 235–6.

p. 35: 'Then she spoke her own poems . . .' Ibid., pp. 236–7.

'showed no sign . . .', 'The door opened . . .' Ibid., p. 238.

p. 36: 'it was plain . . .', 'he had been allowed . . .' Ibid.

p. 37: 'I can say . . .' IB, 'Notes on a Visit to Leningrad', § 13, p. 5.

p. 38: 'addressee and hero . . .' Title of an article by Leonid Zykov:

'Nikolay Punin – adresat i geroy liriki Anny Akhmatovoy', *Zvezda* 1/1996, pp. 77–114.

pp. 38–9: 'The "Guest from the Future" . . .' Mandelstam, p. 360.

p. 40: 'The meeting defined . . .' Nayman, p. 109.

p. 41: 'Thus, torn . . .' AA, *Cinque*, 1, 26 November 1945, translated by Hemschemeyer, II, p. 235.

'That late-night dialogue . . .' AA, *Cinque*, 2, 20 December 1945, ibid., p. 237.

p. 42: 'Not on the leaf-strewn asphalt . . .' AA, *Midnight Verses*, 6: 'The Visit at Night', 10–13 September 1963, ibid., p. 275.

'This black and everlasting separation . . .' AA, *Sweetbrier in Blossom*, 3: 'In a Dream', 15 February 1946, ibid., p. 243.

pp. 42–3: 'Away with time . . .' AA, *Sweetbrier in Blossom*, 2: 'In Reality', 13 June 1946, ibid.

pp. 43–4: 'For so long I hated . . .' AA, *Cinque*, 3, 20 December 1945, ibid., p. 237.

p. 44: 'As the night wore on . . .' IB, 1998, pp. 240, 242.

p. 45: 'Neither despair, nor shame . . .' AA, *Cinque*, 1, translated by McKane, p. 189.

'And that door . . .' AA, *Cinque*, 1, translated by Hemschemeyer, II, p. 235.

p. 46: 'Then she began . . .', 'In memory of all . . .' Vilenkin, p. 268.

'*The guest from the future! Is it possible? . . .*' AA, *Poem Without a Hero*, Part One, Chapter One, lines 91–3, first draft, here translated by Wood.

'*The guest from the future! – Is it true . . .*' Ibid., final draft, translated by Hemschemeyer, II, p. 417.

p. 47: 'People called out . . .' Vilenkin, p. 268.

'When the public . . .' Ibid., p. 522.

'life seems politically easier . . .', 'The writers . . .', 'Present freedom of circulation . . .' IB, 'Notes on a Visit to Leningrad', § 6, p. 2; § 17, p. 7; ibid.

p. 48: 'the difference between Communists . . .' Ibid., p. 6.

'Over the entire scene . . .', 'Writers, who are generally considered . . .' IB, 'A Note on Literature and the Arts . . .', pp. 8, 6.

p. 49: 'They hoped . . .', 'I obtained the general impression . . .'

IB, 'Notes on a Visit to Leningrad', § 16, pp. 6–7; § 14, p. 6.

p. 50: 'In spite of your most persuasive letter . . .' Richard Livingstone, Corpus Christi College, Oxford, to IB, 1 June 1946.

'the poetess . . .' IB to Frank Roberts, British Embassy, Moscow, 20 February 1946.

pp. 51–2: 'When Akhmatova was here . . .' Boris Pasternak to IB, 26 June 1946, here translated from the Russian by Dr Julie Curtis.

2 EXCOMMUNICATION

p. 53: 'When she appeared . . .' Vilenkin, p. 119.

'I visited the poet . . .' AA, January 1914, translated by Hemschemeyer, I, p. 363.

p. 54: 'Threatening clouds . . .' Aleksey Surkov, poem from *Stikhotvoreniya* [Poems], Moscow, 1950.

'This was an encounter . . .' Vilenkin, p. 119.

p. 55: 'We felt exceedingly apprehensive . . .' Chukovskaya, II, 1997, p. 10.

pp. 55–6: 'The historic premises . . .' Ibid.

pp. 56–7: 'I come now . . .' *Pravda* no. 225, 21 September 1946.

p. 57: 'un-Soviet writer . . .' Ibid.

p. 58: 'I have always sympathized . . .' Mikhail Zoshchenko, 'Zavoyevaniya kultury' [The gains of culture], 1926.

'I can always tell a foreigner . . .' Id., 'Inostranets' [The foreigner], 1931.

p. 59: 'I come now to my conclusion . . .' Id., 'Rech' pravdoma po sluchayu yubilyeya stoletiya so dnya smerti Pushkina' [Speech by the chairman of a housing cooperative on the occasion of the centenary of Pushkin's death], 1938.

p. 60: 'in which Akhmatova . . .' *Pravda* no. 225, 21 September 1946.

'And I swear to you . . .' AA, July 1921, translated by McKane, p. 100.

p. 61: 'Here already we can see . . .' Boris Eikhenbaum, *Anna*

Akhmatova: opyt analiza [Anna Akhmatova: an experimental analysis], St Petersburg, 1922, p. 114.

p. 63: 'The rubbish that Akhmatova . . .', 'It really is a disgrace . . .' Babichenko, pp. 51, 53.

p. 64: 'She meant it . . .' IB with author, August 1995.

p. 65: 'Long enough . . .' AA, Third and Last [Dedication] to *Poem Without a Hero*, 5 January 1956, translated by Hemschemeyer, II, p. 407.

p. 67: 'In my opinion . . .' Mandelstam, p. 307.

p. 68: 'The prophetically inclined . . .' Vilenkin, p. 522.

'Here I am earning . . .' Chukovskaya, III, 1997.

pp. 69–70: '*Prokofiev* . . . As far as the poems . . .' Babichenko, p. 50.

p. 73: 'In this opera . . .' Zhdanov, 1948.

pp. 73–4: 'Some people find . . .' *Pravda* no. 225, 21 September 1946.

p. 74: 'In the year 1943 . . .' Babichenko, p. 132.

p. 75: 'We fought . . .' Ibid., p. 171.

p. 76: 'Good God! . . .' Vilenkin, p. 504.

'Just put up with it . . .' Chukovskaya, II, 1997, p. 69.

'They kept saying . . .' Vilenkin, p. 468.

p. 77: 'I was on holiday . . .' Ibid., p. 270.

p. 79: 'The subject Akhmatova . . .' *Gosbezopasnost' i literatura*, p. 77.

pp. 79–80: 'Poor people . . .' Ibid.

p. 80: 'a woman who has been born . . .' Chukovskaya, III, 1997, p. 465.

'Akhmatova's memory . . .' Mandelstam, p. 294.

p. 82: 'You can say one thing . . .' Babichenko, p. 251.

'[Edward] Crankshaw . . .' Iván Boldizsár, *Fortochka*, Budapest, 1948.

p. 83: 'I'm studying the history . . .', 'It didn't do anything . . .' Babichenko, pp. 242, 251.

'It is well known . . .' Kuzmina, p. 242.

p. 84: 'Akuma lay . . .' Vilenkin, p. 471.

p. 85: 'You will have been in a state . . .' 'N.', British Embassy, Madrid to IB, 3 October 1946.

'well and living happily . . .' Brenda Tripp, London, to IB, 12
    February 1947.
'Anna A. has been allowed . . .' 'Anna', Moscow, to IB, 19
    February 1947.
pp. 85–6: 'Otherwise, as far as BL . . .' Ibid.
p. 87: 'Anna Andreyevna . . .' Vilenkin, p. 359.
p. 88: 'For seventeen months . . .' AA, *Requiem*, V, 1939, trans-
    lated by Hemschemeyer, II, p. 103.
p. 90: 'could be of no . . .', 'They are indifferent poems . . .'
    Rossiysky Tsentr . . ., f. 5, op. 16, d. 395.
p. 91: 'We don't want . . .' IB with author, August 1995.

3 'OXFORD' STUDENTS IN LENINGRAD

p. 94: 'Recently I have . . .' Chukovskaya, 1993, p. 90.
'I've been to see Fedin . . .' Chukovsky, p. 205.
p. 97: *Visit from Moscow* . . .' Adolf Endler, 'Besuch aus Moskau
    1954', *Akte Endler* [The Endler file], Peckham, Leipzig, 1978.
'We stayed at the Metropol . . .' Shukman with author, August
    1995.
p. 98: 'It's Orwell and Trotsky . . .' Ibid.
p. 99: 'You absolutely have . . .' Chukovskaya, 1993, p. 113.
pp. 99–100: 'They sent a car . . .' Ibid., pp. 113, 114.
pp. 100–1: 'The discussion lasted . . .' Rossiysky Tsentr . . ., f. 5,
    op. 17, r. 5719.
p. 101: 'I knew a catastrophe . . .' Chukovskaya, II, 1997, p. 73.
p. 102: 'Eight years later . . .' Gerstein, 1989, p. 107.
'Mikhail Mikhaylovich . . .' Chukovskaya, 1993, p. 107.
p. 103: 'What could I . . .' Zoshchenko, p. 182.
p. 104: 'It is said . . .' Mandelstam, p. 294.
p. 105: 'What sort of English people . . .' Chukovskaya, 1993,
    p. 114.
'the misplaced well-wishing . . .' Haight, p. 162.
p. 106: 'The situation in the . . .' Shukman with author, August
    1995.
pp. 106–7: 'She stayed at this hotel . . .' Ibid.
p. 108: 'When you're wearing ermine . . .' Vilenkin, p. 155.

pp. 109–10: 'It must be pointed out . . .' Rossiysky Tsentr . . ., f. 5, r. 5719, op. 17.

p. 110: 'Those present . . .' Zoshchenko, p. 181.

pp. 110–11: 'A visit to the famous . . .' Claudio Véliz, 'A Student in the USSR', *New Statesman and Nation*, 7 August 1954.

p. 111: 'Talking to people . . .' Zoshchenko, p. 186.

pp. 112–13: 'Mikhail Mikhaylovich . . .' Chukovskaya, 1993, p. 108.

p. 113: 'I asked him about Mama . . .' Gerstein, 1995 (2), p. 156.

4   THE NON-MEETING

p. 116: 'How can such a parasite . . .', 'He was at Zhdanov's side . . .' Chukovsky, pp. 223–4.

p. 117: 'And *Yegolin* . . .' Chukovskaya, II, 1997, p. 229.

p. 120: 'Is it true . . .' Chukovskaya, 1993, p. 136.

p. 121: 'She never actually . . .' Gumilyov, p. 132.

p. 122: 'My mother always told me . . .' *Gosbezopasnost' i literatura*, p. 75.

'I shall probably astonish . . .' Gerstein, 1995 (1), pp. 153, 154.

pp. 123–4: 'Pasternak told me . . .' IB, 1998, pp. 243–4.

p. 124: 'but she [AA] . . .' Ibid., p. 244.

p. 125: 'The cause of the "Non-Meeting" . . .' Mandelstam, p. 298.

pp. 125–6: 'The friendly service . . .' Gerstein, 1995 (1), p. 153.

pp. 126–7: 'Later that day . . .' IB, 1998, p. 244.

p. 127: 'A man called me . . .', 'Although her words . . .' Chukovskaya, 1993, pp. 154–5.

p. 129: 'O my August . . .' AA, *The Sweetbriar in Bloom* [*Sweetbrier in Blossom*], 6: 'A Dream', 14 August 1956, translated by McKane, pp. 193–4.

'"reproachfully"': '"Can things . . ." . . .' Chukovskaya, 1993, p. 152.

'It was in everything . . .' AA, *Sweetbrier in Blossom*, 6: 'A Dream', translated by Hemschemeyer, II, p. 247.

p. 130: 'How shall I pay back . . .' *The Sweetbriar in Bloom*

[*Sweetbrier in Blossom*], 6: 'A Dream', translated by McKane, p. 194.

'You invented me . . .' Ibid., 8, p. 194.

p. 131: 'Both of them . . .' Chukovskaya, 1993, p. 157.

p. 132: 'The celebrations . . .' AA, *The Sweetbriar in Bloom* [*Sweetbrier in Blossom*], 4: 'First Song', 1956, translated by McKane, p. 192 (first seven lines) and Hemschemeyer, II, p. 245 (last line).

'He won't become . . .' AA, *Poem Without a Hero*, Third and Last [Dedication], 5 January 1956, translated by McKane, p. 291.

'Dear friend . . .' AA, quoted from Gerstein, 1995 (1), here translated by Wood.

p. 133: 'It was a mistake . . .' AA, 'From an Italian Diary', 1964, translated by McKane, p. 234.

'At least today . . .' AA, 9 June 1958, translated by Hemschemeyer, II, p. 651.

'It's a long time . . .' AA, 24 October 1959, here translated by Wood.

p. 136: 'Among the greatest problems . . .', 'There are *some* writers . . .' Chukovskaya, II, 1997, pp. 667, 669.

p. 137: 'The opera shows us . . .' Zhdanov, 10 February 1948.

p. 139: 'In the Literature Faculty . . .', 'The Resolution on the journals . . .' *Voprosy Literatury* 1/1994, p. 273, 274.

p. 140: 'At the same time . . .' Ibid.

p. 141: 'she had reread Chekhov . . .', 'his universe was . . .' IB, 1998, pp. 244, 231.

p. 143: 'The point is this . . .' and all prose quotations on pp. 144 and 145: Chekhov, *Ward No. 6*, 1892.

'I do not live . . .' AA, 1958, here translated by Wood.

pp. 146–7: 'Object is in Moscow . . .' *Gosbezopasnost' i literatura*, pp. 78–9.

5   LATE FAME

p. 148: 'I consider it . . .' Rossiysky Tsentr . . ., f. 5, op. 30, r. 465.3.

p. 149: 'In those years . . .', 'Some form of *State* . . .' Ibid.

p. 153: 'You can ignore . . .' Chukovskaya, II, 1997, p. 552.

pp. 153–4: 'necessity of reassessing . . .', 'unsuitable to repeat . . .' Rossiysky Tsentr . . ., f. 5, op. 36, r. 5851.

p. 154: 'It is well known . . .' Ibid., f. 4, op. 18, r. 3638.

'get on with the work . . .' Ibid., f. 5, op. 55, r. 7741.

p. 155: 'in view of the special . . .', '*Zvezda* was sharply criticized . . .' Ibid.

p. 156: 'we are obliged . . .' Ibid.

p. 157: 'You will write . . .' Epigraph (J. Brodsky) to AA, 'The Last Rose', 9 August 1962, translated by McKane, p. 225.

p. 158: 'It was curious . . .' Bongard, 1963.

'She liked to know . . .' Vilenkin, pp. 363–4.

'She repeated this . . .' Chukovskaya, II, 1997, p. 543.

p. 159: 'Don't torment . . .', 'And don't ask God . . .' AA, December 1921, translated by Hemschemeyer, I, p. 545.

p. 160: 'Now, however, Akhmatova . . .' Vilenkin, p. 591.

pp. 160–1: 'She received us . . .' Bongard, 1963.

pp. 161–2: '*He speaks:* / Dear sister . . .' AA, 'Prologue: A Play', 1940s, translated by McKane, p. 258.

p. 162: 'Akhmatova always spoke . . .' Nayman, *Novy Mir*, 1989.

'She has known Isaiah Berlin . . .' Vilenkin, pp. 645–6.

'Anna Akhmatova told me . . .' Ivanov, p. 202.

p. 163: 'Yesterday Anna Akhmatova called . . .' Chukovsky, p. 372.

p. 164: 'She began to question me . . .' Chukovskaya, 1993, pp. 70–1.

'Flattering, isn't it?' Ibid., p. 71.

p. 165: 'If these sinister individuals . . .' György Dalos, *Prophet zum Produzenten*, Wespennest, Vienna, 1992, p. 88.

p. 166: 'was of pro-Soviet . . .' Nayman, Moscow, 1989, p. 183.

p. 167: 'All those not expected . . .' AA, 1957/8, translated by Hemschemeyer, II, p. 649.

pp. 168–9: 'her former husband . . .' Rossiysky Tsentr . . ., f. 5, op. 30, r. 4653.

p. 170: 'It appears from . . .', 'Despite the fact . . .' Ibid., f. 5, op. 55, r. 7741.

pp. 170–1: 'Under the circumstances . . .' Ibid.

p. 171: 'Akhmatova to Italy . . .' Chukovsky, p. 362.

pp. 171–2: 'I'm going on this trip . . .' Orlova and Kopelev, p. 105.

p. 172: 'Even if I had known Christ . . .' Richter, 1965.

pp. 172–3: 'The trip was worth it . . .' Lakshin, p. 259.

p. 173: 'Ah, Italian Communism . . .' Richter, 1965.

pp. 174–5: 'When at night . . .' AA, 'The Muse', 1924, translated by Hemschemeyer, II, pp. 73, 75.

p. 175: 'Yes, she read in Russian . . .' Richter, 1965.

p. 176: 'Dawn breaks . . .' AA, 'From the Diary of a Journey', December 1964, translated by McKane, p. 245.

'Joseph . . .' AA, *Sochineniya v dvukh tomakh* [Works in two volumes], Izd. Pravda, Moscow, 1990, II, p. 253.

pp. 176–7: 'Fame's high threshold . . . forewarned me': AA, *The Way of All the Earth*, March 1940, translated by McKane, p. 277.

p. 177: 'What a biography . . .' Nayman, *Novy Mir*, 1989, p. 162.

p. 178: 'No, thank you . . .' Vilenkin, p. 620.

'When will the Soviet Union . . .' Chukovskaya, II, 1997, p. 543.

6   HONORIS CAUSA

p. 179: 'It will, I think, be best . . .', 'to dear Miss Brenda Tripp . . .' IB, Headington House, Oxford, to Bowra, 27 October 1964.

pp. 179–80: 'The University of Oxford . . .' The Registrar, Oxford University to AA (telegram), 3 November 1964.

p. 180: 'there would be no difficulty . . .' F.H. Sandford (Registrar, Oxford University) to AA, 3 November 1964.

p. 181: 'with gratitude . . .', 'it depends . . .' AA to Sandford, 1 December 1964.

'We send you . . .' Sir Paul Sinker, British Council, London to AA, 16 December 1964; Rossiysky Tsentr . . ., f. 5, op. 50, r. 9423.

pp. 181–2: 'In view of the fact . . .' AA to Aleksey Surkov, 21 February 1965; ibid.

p. 182: 'I have no disagreements . . .' AA, quoted by Alan Moray Williams, *Oxford Mail*, 26 January 1965.

p. 183: 'excerpt from the minutes'. Rossiysky Tsentr . . ., f. 5, op. 50, r. 9423.

p. 184: '*16 May 1965* . . .' Chukovsky, pp. 371, 372.

'What are they thinking? . . .' Nayman, Moscow, 1989.

'contained slanders against . . .', 'a cycle of poems . . .' Rossiysky Tsentr . . ., f. 5, op. 33, r. 4821.

p. 185: 'If an invitation . . .' *Daily Telegraph*, 3 June 1965.

p. 186: 'Some years after . . .' Rossiysky Tsentr . . ., f. 5, op. 50, r. 9423.

pp. 188–9: '*3 June* . . . Akhmatova's name . . .' Vilenkin, pp. 659–61.

p. 191: 'All the other poets . . .' Nayman, Moscow, 1989, pp. 26–7.

p. 192: 'From the year nineteen-forty . . .' AA, *Poem Without a Hero*, Introduction, 25 August 1941, translated by McKane, p. 292.

pp. 192–3: 'the allusions might be . . .', 'She answered that when . . .' IB, 1998, pp. 248–9.

p. 193: 'tortured mouth . . .' AA, *Requiem*, Epilogue, 2, March 1940, here translated by McKane and Wood.

'Because in our harsh age . . .' Alexander Pushkin, 'I have built . . .', 1836.

pp. 193–4: 'After her return . . .' Nayman, *Novy Mir*, 1989.

p. 194: 'Lady Berlin . . .' Chukovsky, p. 315.

'Not to a secret pavilion . . .' AA, 5 August 1965, translated by Hemschemeyer, II, p. 737.

p. 195: 'Pray, at night . . .' AA, 1965, ibid., p. 741.

'*On your account* . . .' AA, *Poem Without a Hero*, Epilogue, lines 43–4, here translated by Wood.

'had she come across . . .' IB, 1998, p. 246.

p. 196: 'O Lord! . . .' AA, 'The Last Rose', 9 August 1962, translated by McKane, p. 225.

7   EARTHLY AND HEAVENLY JUSTICE

pp. 200–1: 'that the said Resolution . . .' Rossiysky Tsentr . . ., f. 3, op. 103, r. 153.

p. 204: 'The cunning moon . . .' AA, *The Sweetbriar in Bloom* [*Sweetbrier in Blossom*], 13, 1946, translated by McKane, p. 197.

pp. 207–8: 'People never like . . .' Lyudmila Karachkina, Crimean Astrophysical Observatory, Nauchny, faxed letter to author, 20 September 1995.

Index